Silver Streak Revisited

A Collection of
Essays, Adventures, and Misadventures

By

Emily O'Neil Bott

This Book is Dedicated

First to my children, Brian, Eric, Kathy, Martha, Daniel, Aimee and Sarah, whose adventures provided so much of the material.

The grandchildren are close in line: Zach and Kale Platt, Deva, Sadhu, Markandeya and Ananta Bott, Montana and Carson Murphy. And a new great-granddaughter, Imani Morin, who doesn't yet realize the fun that lies ahead in this life.

May they be loved, at peace in their choices, and not afraid to take risks.

l. to r. – Kathy, Eric, Aimee, Daniel, Martha and Brian holding Sarah.

Thank you

To Tom Stevens for the photos of the sinking car, and for writing classes that fueled the imagination.

To Paul Wood, who prodded me to put these columns into a book, and who graciously helped with much-needed advice.

To Sarah Bott, computer whiz, who pulled me out of many a hole.

To Aimee Joyaux for creating the cover.

But the whole mess would still be strewn about my floor if it weren't for Sally Simonds, who served as editor, adviser, and chief of morale.
"Don't stress out. We can do this!"

Silver Streak Revisited is available at

https://www.createspace.com/3820034

and

amazon.com

Swallow that Car

I own a twelve by fifteen foot chunk of Queen Ka'ahumanu Shopping Center's parking lot. Actually I don't own it, but, in September of 1974, I rented it for a couple of harrowing hours when it swallowed my car.

The freak incident took place with a little help from my son Eric while I was eating lunch in the Liberty House personnel lounge. The store was barely two years old, and all the employees knew each other. We welcomed the opportunity to get off our feet, grab our brown bags out of the refrigerator and talk story.

Our chatter was interrupted by a knock on the door. It was Eric. "Mom, can I borrow the car? I need new shoes." He was on the track team at Baldwin, so it was a reasonable request even though I was extremely protective of that car. Not only was it the first major purchase I had made since a recent divorce, but a symbol of independence. Without transportation it would be next to impossible to earn a living.

The red station wagon was almost a member of the family. It took us to sunrises at Haleakala, weekends at Waianapanapa, and regular treks to the beach. And it held a lot of groceries to feed a lot of kids.

I was more than a little skittish about lending it, so, along with the keys Eric got the safety lecture. What I neglected to tell him was that I hadn't parked in the usual space. "Just wait. He'll be back," I predicted. On schedule a few minutes later the door burst open.

"Mom, you're not gonna believe what happened to the car!"

"What? Did it move, hah hah?"

"It fell in a hole, Mom, and it's in the water."

"It WHAT?"

"It fell in the water, Mom, I swear."

"What water? What are you taking about?" Clearly he was upset.

What I mistook for a smirk was actually shock. "The water, Mom, it fell in a hole, and there's water."

I was out the door, job or no job.

There, not twenty yards from the store's side entrance, was my little red station wagon, headed for the basement. Except there was no basement. The Golf lay drunkenly tilting backwards, drowning in a pool of murky water, which churned halfway up

6

the rear window. Only the left front wheel, clinging to the asphalt, kept it from being submerged.

Photo by Tom Stevens

By now a crowd had gathered, including security, police, and camera-laden Tom Stevens from the Maui News. Eric was basking in attention, but I was frantic.

7

How would we get home? Who would pay for this? Could the car be salvaged? Would it smell? And for heaven's sake, what had happened in the first place?

As he explained it, Eric had no trouble locating the vehicle, but when he started to reverse out of the parking space, the back end of the car went down. And down. He jumped out into a rapidly rising pool of water that hadn't been there when he unlocked the door.

"It was like quicksand. The thing just kept sinking."

It turned out a broken pipe under the pavement had been spewing water, displacing the sand, gravel, and whatever else was beneath the surface. When my son moved the wagon, its weight caused the asphalt to collapse.

Store manager Judith Cohen assured me we would not be left in the lurch. The shopping center's insurance would be glad to provide transportation, starting immediately.

With the main valve shut off, the water slowly receded. A tow truck groaned the vehicle back to the surface. The car was deemed a total wreck.

We drove home that night in a set of rental wheels, to be replaced by "something comparable" to the dear departed. I must say the shopping center personnel took very good care of us, but I hated to see that car dragged away. It had been a real friend in need.

A few weeks later I didn't know whether to laugh or cry when I spotted the car back on the road. The tow truck operator had bought it from the insurance company, hosed it down, wiped it off, and aired it out.

He drove it happily for years.

My kids used to refer to the newly repaved spot as "the Bott Mom memorial space." But I never parked there again.

There's such a thing as tempting fate.

A Christmas Story

Thank you, Sir, whoever you are. You gifted me with the defining moment of Christmas, 2004. And you probably don't even know it.

It was a busy morning at the Salvation Army kettle. Tourists, fresh off the cruise ship, stretched their legs and looked for bargains in the Maui Mall.

Aside from young mothers with children, the local crowd was pretty much the over- seventy variety. A few of them braved rubber slippers and shorts, but most people huddled in their once-a-year sweaters, shivering in the unaccustomed chill wind.

The cool air didn't affect their generosity. The kettle outside Longs Drugs was experiencing what one wag called "a silent collection", lots of dollar bills, accompanied by lots of smiles and wishes for a happy holiday. The little kids got a big thrill out of ringing the bell, as I crossed my fingers and assured them Santa was watching and they were being "very good."

About halfway through the morning the Maui Economic Opportunity bus pulled up to discharge its clients, the majority of whom were old or feeble or both. The operator, God bless her, took her job very seriously. Passengers were helped to the pavement with great care.

Finally the last man debarked, after the driver had placed his walker within reach at the foot of the steps. He was frail to the point of wispy, and his tentative gait made it obvious that walking was painful. But he smiled as he shuffled toward the store, seeming to enjoy my attempt at playing the ukulele.

Pausing for breath, he nodded when I asked, "Silent Night?"

"Yes. I know it in German." Was he a G.I. in World War II? Yes. He had learned the song from an instructor who spoke the language.

With energy at a premium, he went directly into Longs. "I only have a little time. The bus comes back on schedule."

To my surprise, he reappeared almost immediately, obviously disappointed. Even that little activity, in such a crowded environment, had proved too much. He had no packages. There would be no shopping today.

What could be done? The man was alone. Maybe some music would cheer him up. Strumming the only three chords I knew, I walked a few steps with him and sang, "Silent night, holy night."

His face lit up as he chimed in. *"Stille nacht, heil'ge nacht."* All the way through that lovely carol, we managed a shaky, bilingual duet.

His smile was a gift I treasure. A photograph would have been superfluous. For a few shining moments, he was twenty-one and strong again.

Whoever you were, Sir, thank you. You were all the Christmas I need.

Haleakala Times (2004) A version of this also appeared in "Catholic Digest"

Aimee's Barometer

"No, no, no!" I was frantically hissing to my daughter. She was standing at the driver's window, and I was behind the cab...if, indeed, it was a cab. There was no dome light, I couldn't see a fare box, and there were two people in the front seat. Was Aimee so anxious to get back to the hotel that she was setting us up to be driven out in the country and left for dead?

My daughter kept waving me off. Finally she walked back and whispered: "Trust me, Mom. There is a fare box. And, bedsides, I have a good shit barometer."

"You have a what?"

"Never mind. Just trust me. I'll explain later." And so began one of our most interesting experiences in a three-week trip.

We had spent the day touring Toronto, and had decided on the spur of the moment to take the elevator to the top of the CN Tower, reputed to be the tallest freestanding building in the world. How long would we have to wait? About fifteen minutes, according to the ticket agent. But you have to take two elevators. As the tower narrows, only eight people can fit into the "lift" for the final ascent.

Hah! Half an hour later we were in the observatory, three quarters of the way up, drinking in the sunset and the ever-darkening silhouette of the city. There was nothing but a chain link fence between us and the North Pole. But the long line in front of the second elevator meant several hours in that cramped atmosphere. A single exchanged look and we were on the way back down. By the time we reached ground level it was too dark and we were too tired to walk back to the hotel. And there was not a cab in sight. Only this one car with a driver anxious to give us a ride.

Aimee was talking with him, and seemed to have things under control. It's a funny thing, but after my kids left Maui, they had amazing adventures all over the world. So I've learned to trust their judgement. After she struck a bargain with the driver, things calmed down. His lilting accent got us guessing his country of origin. He gave us hints. An island. Calypso. When we broke into

"Hey, Mr. Tally man, tally me banana," he cracked up and the floodgates opened. The other passenger turned out to be his sister. He had already brought eighteen family members to

Toronto, putting them up in his own home until they got their feet on the ground.

His story was so bizarre that I secretly had my doubts. Friend of a cabinet member? He fished out a snapshot of them playing golf. Youngest daughter graduating with honors? Her program was in the glove compartment.

Aimee does, indeed have a good barometer.

All Colors, All Styles

Last year at about this time, my daughter Kathy asked me to pick up her first grader, Kale, at his elementary school.

Standing under the overhang, I reflected on a ten-year period, long ago in another life, during which I enrolled seven successive children in first grade. I recalled waiting for the dismissal bell at nine schools in five different states. Years and years of PTA meetings, miles and miles of varnished floors. Hours of teachers' conferences, Hallowe'en costumes, school trips, picnics, bake sales, soccer, football, swimming practice, softball, ice hockey, track, recitals. Christmas plays, emergency trips to various hospitals, homework. Building volcanos on the kitchen table; ski trips and class picnics. The full gamut of childhood activities.

Crew cuts were in style then, too. Funny how things repeat themselves. But there were subtle differences. The mothers at Kula Elementary School seemed younger, more like teen-age baby sitters. They moved restlessly about the covered walkway with that easy grace that seems to belong to the young. I was struck by the sheer beauty of them. Theirs seemed a dream world in which no one had problems. No one was sick. They all had shining hair; bright, clear faces; erect posture. Their handsome toddlers staggered happily about, not too far from Mama, waiting expectantly for the clang that would announce Big Sibling was free for the weekend.

Then the sharp, wake-the-dead noise so loved by school kids everywhere: the dismissal bell. The energy level on the lanai ratcheted up a few decibels as the Tiny Tims humphed up the stairs, grasping lunch bags in their little paws, tiny backpacks attached to their tiny backs. All Grown Up, going home to where they really lived. Some were self-confident, born for adventure; a few hung back, not too sure about all this.

Another bell, another building erupted. BIG kids bounded out, some pulling themselves along outside the railing. King of the hill. Outta my way, dude. A tornado of energy, yet with a reassuring, positive quality about it. No shoving, no ugliness. Just beautiful kids. All colors, all styles, all Maui. God, how lucky we are.

Then, Bingo. Kale Colossal (as he calls himself), struggled up the stairs weighted down by backpack, lunch sack and fierce bear. Well, not so fierce. A construction paper face, lovingly made by hand and threatening to come unglued. Six is such a great age. So trustful. Such an innocent dignity.

13

"Hi, Tutu, can we get a treat on the way home?" Mr. Casual.

Thud. Back to earth I came, out of dreamland. Or was I? I'll hold this dream for a long, long while. Want me to pick him up again, Kathy? Any time.

Kihei Times, September 22, 1998

Aloha, Welcome to Maui

They pour off the cruise ship in waves, anxious to play golf or find a beach or simply explore the island. They're passengers on the liners that dock in Kahului every Monday and Friday and they're ready to go.

I'm new at the job of greeter, but so far it's been a hoot. Tourists getting off the Pride of Aloha or Pride of America seem to be having a wonderful time. For many, it's their first trip to the Islands. These are not the sophisticated travelers who book the Queen Elizabeth II. These are the average Joes who probably thought long and hard before planning this trip.

Security is tight at the harbor. Greeters (there are as many as four a shift) have to park outside the fence and sign in at the gate. Two badges are required: a photo ID from the Maui Visitors Bureau and a card that proves we've attended Security Awareness Training. The parking lot is crammed with tour buses and car rental vans. Taxis are lined up outside the gate. Once inside the terminal, we pick up baskets of pins that proclaim "I (heart) Maui" and, as the job says, greet passengers.

The building itself is just a big shed. We are not allowed past the gates to the actual dock. Occasionally the sound of the metal detector is heard as a passenger or crew member goes through security on the way back to the ship. I would guess this creates a long line as departure time approaches.

There's a stage at one end of the building, with rows of chairs for passengers to rest while listening to Joe Bommarito and Sheldon Brown play Hawaiian music and banter with the guests. Joe's wife, Joann, learned hula from Gordean Bailey. I suspect the audience might not realize this is an exceptional show. Some passengers are drawn instead to the vendors' tables, where jewelry, clothing, yarn lei and Hawaiian trinkets are for sale.

It's not hard to greet visitors with a smile along with a pin, because most of them are so receptive. They love the whole concept. Many ask for extra buttons to take home for friends. Some repeat our "Aloha" over and over. Entire families, car seats, strollers and all, head for the parking lot. You can hear snatches of conversations. I was surprised to hear two people discussing plans to visit Walmart.

Occasionally a young person hurries off, skateboard in hand. Or a determined athlete pushes a mountain bike. Another carries snorkel fins. Crew members?

15

If baseball caps or tee shirts are any indication, passengers come from every place imaginable, and a few unimaginable. They proclaim The Salty Dog, Martha's Vineyard; Pittsburgh Senior Men's Basketball; Bohannan Mountain Volunteer Fire Dept., Wesley, AR; Westlake Football, Austin TX; Señor Frogs, Cozumel, Mexico; Hibriten Baseball, Lenoir. There's Ride Hard-Lake Powell; Grapevine, TX, and my current favorite, To save time, let's just assume I know everything.

It's not just the tee shirts that tell a story. This morning an entire wedding party appeared, the men sweating in tuxedos, the bride absolutely gorgeous in her white gown and veil. I silently prayed they had arranged for air conditioned transportation. The rain had stopped, but the humidity was just starting.

Another interesting group in today's mix was a 50-member symphony band from Ridgecrest High School in Southern California. In addition to being in tuxedos or long black dresses, some were lugging heavy instruments. All were rushing to get on buses. They were headed upcountry to play for Kamehameha School Maui. I was sorry they didn't have time to stop for a while and listen to our Hawaiian music.

It's a fun couple of hours. Our little harbor is just a speck among the 96,000 miles of open shoreline in the United States. But it sees a lot of happy people. How can you not like a job where a little old man takes your I (heart) Maui pin, smiles, and says, "I'd like to take you home with me"?

Haleakala Times, March 29-April 11 2006

Christmas Memories

What's your best Christmas memory? Chances are it has more to do with people than price.

Two of my strongest recollections are bittersweet. At age six, I opened a copy of The House at Pooh Corner, inscribed "with Love from Santa Claus." Nobody in the whole world scrawled like my father. He had unwittingly ended my innocence.

The second mixed blessing happened during the Depression, when money was so tight that the family car was up on blocks. I had given up hoping for the only thing I really wanted, a bicycle. My cousin and I were poking around his basement when we stumbled across a two-wheeler that had been patched up and repainted bright green. It was my size, not his. I didn't know whether to laugh or cry. It wasn't much of a bike, but it was a lot of love.

Years later my older sister visited with her husband and toddler son. With a two year old to spoil, we single aunties and uncles went wild. He was the first grandchild, and we were in foreign territory. What to get him? Everything. On the big morning, my sister gently steered him to the pile of clowns and games, toys and dolls, bears and books. The rest of us sent frantic signals: "Pick mine first." For a minute he stared, uncomprehending. Then, ignoring the best money could buy, he reached past the wagon, the tricycle, the rocking chair, and grabbed a red toothbrush. And so it goes.

A lifetime later, my father-in-law would apologize for sending a Christmas check instead of presents. To us it wasn't money. It was his (and our) way of getting the children something special from Grandpa.

Of course, there were the inevitable glitches. One year my husband and I came home with identical basketballs. Then there was the time the fourth spring wouldn't fit on the Wonder Horse until well past midnight.

Some years it wasn't so much the gift as how it was used. Long ago, new blue jeans were so stiff they'd practically stand up by themselves. Our teenagers broke in their Christmas pants by wearing them body-surfing.

One of my friends recalls her mother pointing out the red light atop a radio tower. The kids believed it was Rudolph. Later, as she and her brother soaked in the tub, Grandma slammed and banged about in the living room, calling "Ho! Ho! Ho!" Mom pretended to rush the frantic children out of the bath, but, of course, they had "just missed" Santa.

And, for deep down, heart warming tugs, there's nothing like having a new infant in your arms on Christmas morning. Two of our children were December babies. That's the best reminder of the reason for the season. If you can't manage that, take comfort in this thought: maybe, just maybe, your best Christmas memory is still ahead.

Country Mice

What special "last things" should we do with the kids before we moved from Connecticut to Michigan? The year was 1963. What wonderful memories would we like to create? Something in the city that we couldn't duplicate in the midwest.

We pored over the New York Times, looking for activities that would trigger nostalgia forever. Aha! The Sound of Music was playing on Broadway. Perfect. We'd leave the three little ones at home with a sitter. I would take seven-year-old Kathy and five-year- old Martha to lunch at Lindy's and then to the play. Bob opted to tour an ocean liner with Brian, 11, and Eric, nine. Hmmmm. That sounded like a lot of fun. For a split second, I wavered. Could we possibly do both?

The day dawned rainy and cold. We were late. Traffic was worse than expected, and we arrived in Manhattan with the adults edgy and the kids restless. The script began to fall apart.

Lindy's was packed. We were late. What was the quickest thing on the menu? Sandwiches, of course. The same thing we ate the other 364 days of the year. No matter. These were glamorous restaurant sandwiches. Kathy wanted chicken, but at two dollars it was a bit pricey for our budget. Martha chose salami, and we settled for that. Big mistake.

I kept trying to psych the girls up with the glamour of our surroundings. Frank Sinatra ate here. They were not impressed. My reverie was interrupted as Martha asked in a loud voice: "What are these cloth things?" Cloth things? Migod, she meant the napkins! How embarrassing. "Can I take mine home?" Martha again. Death, where is thy sting?

They were too excited to finish the meal. Was that a faint sneer on the waiter's face as he handed us the doggy bag?

Minutes later we were in the nosebleed section of the theater. We settled in. Rather, I settled in. The girls were fidgety. It was hot. I tried burying the lunch remnants under the mound of coats on my lap. (Did you ever realize how much garlic there is in salami?)

As the orchestra warmed up, my mind wandered. Were the guys viewing some fabulous stateroom? Were they having high tea with the captain?

The curtain went up. I was in seventh heaven until the small boy in front of us began rattling his Tootsie Roll wrapper. He tossed the paper to the floor. Martha, loudly: "That boy's a litter!"

19

Oh, how your good deeds come back to haunt you. The mother glared in our direction. I didn't bother trying to apologize. (After all, he WAS a litter.)

Soon after that, Martha again, rummaging about my lap. "I'm hungry." Now it was our turn to rattle paper. The closer it got to the top of the pile, the stronger the sandwich smelled. Hoo boy. Our outing was changing from the Sound of Music to the Scent of Garlic. Why hadn't we just stayed home and listened to the record? I wondered again what the boys were doing.

At last it was over. We did the floor sweep for lost mittens and scarves, and joined the males. It was cold. We were tired.

"So, tell us about your exciting experience. How was the ship? Did you get to go on the bridge? Did you see the lifeboats? The engine room?

They looked glum. "We never saw anything. They wouldn't let us on board on Sunday without a pass. We just wandered around while you were enjoying the play."

Kihei Times, November 10 1998

Disneyland Revisited

I have to stay alive till August 1st to keep a promise made seven years ago. It has to do with Disneyland.

When Number One grandson Zach was goofing off in eighth grade, I told him that I'd bring him and his best pal to Disneyland if he graduated on time. Gracious to Betsy, those are motivating words!

It didn't take a rocket scientist to know I could never keep up with two teenagers. Daughter Kathy had to stay home with Zach's younger brother, Kale, but daughter Sarah was delighted to fly down from Portland to help chaperone. It was almost seven years ago to the day that we arrived in Los Angeles. Being solar powered by nature, I'm used to getting up and going down with the sun. Our flight didn't land until ten-thirty p.m. It was midnight when we got to the hotel, and it took another half hour to switch to a non-smoking suite. Don't ask.

Things were heading downhill. Still awake at three, I was cursing the lack of a sleeping pill. At five-thirty, somebody's mis-set alarm clock went off. I pulled rank and went back to bed, but sleep had fled. The room was too cold with the air conditioner on, and too hot without it. Would this be the vacation from hell?

Several cups of coffee later, life improved. We weren't seasoned Disney folk, like the rest of Maui seemed to be. It was a relief to realize that this was a safe place for Zach and Lawaiah to roam. They could take the early tram to the Park, come back to the hotel for lunch, and ride their little brains out until the place closed down at midnight.

Being fourteen going on twenty, their first stop was a girls' dancing revue. The boys were on the prowl for chicks, none of whom they seemed to meet. (Sarah corrects me on this point: "Mom, we don't know that they didn't. They never would have told us.") We do know that they met their objective of going on all rides at least twice. They were off in their own world of perpetual motion. Sarah joined them occasionally. I found the air-conditioned ice cream parlors and exhibits.

The crowds were humongous. We heard that sixty thousand people come on a normal day. July 4 could top seventy thousand. And hot? Hoo boy. There were terminal sunburns in the making as acres of flesh oozed over tight shorts and hapless halters.

Families in matching tee shirts lined up next to foreign visitors in exotic garb. It was just plain exciting. I was tickled to watch teenagers having their pictures taken with Disney characters. All the pseudo sophistication fell away as small kid memories came to life.

Perhaps the biggest surprise was the realization that my daughter and I had reversed roles. I still wielded the big stick when it came to the boys, but treated her like the adult she was. And she, in turn, became my protector. I found out later that she had been threatened by her siblings with instant death if she let me get overtired. It's great to be old.

Fortunately, we didn't have to use any of the "permission to treat a minor" medical letters we had carried. (Just try getting someone else's child into an ER without them.) Everything went smoothly. The boys accumulated suitcases full of junk, and I gained a pocketful of memories. Sarah enjoyed it so much that she's primed for the encore.

Oh, yes. When we returned to Maui, Zach's seven-year-old brother, Kale, was seriously pouting. He hadn't been invited, and his lower lip went out farther and farther with tales of the fastest this and the scariest that. On the verge of tears, Kale turned to me and whimpered: "Tutu, when do I get to go to Disneyland?"

"When you graduate from eighth grade, like Zach."

"But Tutu, you'll be dead by then."

See why I have to stay alive till August 1st? That's the date we leave.

Eddie's Kids

It's funny how a family snapshot can throw a switch in your memory.

The picture arrived yesterday; my nephew's young family. The boys were carbon copies of their dad. He, in turn, was a clone of my younger brother, Johnny. The male genes ran strong.

It brought me back to World War II when everyone seemed to be in uniform. My university was practically a girl's college, except for the medical and dental schools. Those future officers already wore khaki or navy blue. In my family alone, two brothers and a sister had enlisted, along with four cousins. My proud grandmother honored them with a service flag on her wall, each youngster (and they were youngsters) represented by a bright blue star.

Edging closest to combat was brother Eddie, a brand new Ensign. With his wings of gold, he was practicing carrier techniques at Norfolk Naval Air Station. He sent us a heart-stopping letter describing a near crash during an attempted landing. We prayed this would be his closest call.

His big news followed shortly - a telegram, all in capital letters, typed on slips of paper pasted on a yellow sheet. "Shipping out. Destination Unknown. Don't worry, but bend them knees." We did plenty of both.

He had sent his girlfriend a dozen roses, "With my heart in beside them." He hoped to marry her when he came back. Back from where? When? It was useless to speculate. We kept telling ourselves he would be okay. He had trained for this. This was what he wanted. But the stomach acid flowed.

We lived for mail. We tried to continue "normal" lives. We observed traditions. On Thanksgiving Day, 1942, despite the tension and lack of information, we planned the usual feast.

But early that morning the Western Union boy arrived. Again. This time the telegram wasn't from my brother. This time it was from the Secretary of the Navy. He regretted to inform us that Ensign Robert Edward O'Neil would not be coming home. Ever. No, they didn't send a chaplain and a naval officer, like on tv. They just sent a telegram.

We arranged for the funeral Mass. Monsignor Brinkman asked if we wanted a flag- draped catafalque to represent a coffin. We opted against it. My brother had been blown up at sea. There was no body. Why confuse people?

We tried to pick up the pieces. My grandmother got a new flag, with a gold star. I hated that flag. I didn't need to be reminded.

The hurts didn't stop. A few weeks later his girlfriend's mother phoned, in tears. Her daughter had received birthday flowers from Eddie, and she wanted to know what to do with them. For an insane moment my hopes soared. The nightmare was over. He was alive somewhere on an island. It was all a mistake. No. He had ordered the flowers ahead of time. I could have strangled the woman.

Eight months later we were informed that the President of the United States took pleasure in presenting the Silver Star Medal posthumously to Eddie for conspicuous gallantry and intrepidity as a pilot, delivering a glide-bombing attack against coastal defense gun installations on Table d'Aukaska, Casablanca. We couldn't find Table d'Aukaska on the map. But it didn't matter.

Eventually the war wound down and "ours" came home: sibs Lois and Johnny, cousins Billy, Barbara, Hildegarde, and Tom. The GIs returned, and the wound opened up again and again as Eddie's friends finished college, went to work, married, and got on with their lives. We closed ranks at the dining table, but it wasn't the same.

As I looked at the picture of brother Johnny's handsome son and grandchildren, carrying on his name, I couldn't help but wonder. What would Eddie's kids have been like?

War, the gift that keeps on giving. Just or unjust, it never ends.

Haleakala Times, April 2, 2003

Hip, Hip, Hooray!

Enough with the pills. You've finally decided to head for the Great Palace of Pain and get that miserable hip replaced. My, are you in for some fun. You have sold your body to the cheerleaders. The doctors, the nurses, the physical and occupational therapists, the social workers. All the Good People who will Help You Get Well are now lined up, salivating. By the time they're through, you'll be aware of every imperfection in your frame.

You're weak. You're crooked. One shoulder is lower than the other and you have a drooping right br.... Stop right there.

My surgery took place off-island, but I suspect the drill is pretty much the same everywhere. I wasn't worried. After all, the pamphlets at the doctor's office showed everybody smiling. Even the patients looked happy.

What's to worry about?

Having said that, let me clue you in to a few nuggets that might make your experience less memorable than mine. Get off your sofa right now and load up on frozen food. Buy a "grabber" to pick up all the things you're going to drop.

Break down and get yourself a pedicure. It will be months before you can do anything but glare at those toes. And don't choose dark polish. It looks even uglier as it chips helplessly away.

Get a walker and a cane. They'll wind up crammed under your bed some day, but you'll need them. Have grab bars installed in your bathroom. That's a start.

You're ready for The Knife.

Let me set one rumor to rest. It is not true that you have to walk back from surgery to your room. It's in everyone's best interest to delay physical activity until you've stopped throwing up from the anesthesia. It could be a full ten or twenty minutes before a disembodied voice intones:

"Slide over and stand up." Surely you jest. You have no intention of ever standing again. But these helpers are ruthless. You will stand, by God. And you will grab hold of a walker and lunge around the room. Eventually you'll careen out into the hall, dressed for Hallowe'en.

Your elastic stockings hang beneath the oversized, unisex shorts and saggy half gown. The socks with the pebbly bottoms are crammed into your slippers. The sweater you brought from home is so covered with lint that you're forced to turn it inside out.

25

Hospital chic.

Walking up and down the training steps is tricky, but for sheer terror there's the car. The sweating therapist will wheel you out into the heat and make you, yes make you, practice getting in and out of a parked auto. It's not a pretty sight.

You'll also get to practice a lot of fun exercises. You'll discover that your sore leg can be stretched in new and exciting ways. Not just once, but many times, in directions that probably aren't on the compass.

And no Star Spangled Banner at the end.

The good news? You'll lose weight. It will be mostly in one leg, but a pound is a pound. You might even get to hallucinate. Legally. But that's another story.

The less good news? Your days of plopping down on a soft, low chair to watch TV are over. No more, my love. The new rule is ninety degrees. That means your knees can go no higher than your hips. So you'll learn all sorts of different skills, like putting on your footwear with a long shoehorn, and your socks with an even stranger device.

Be prepared for some changes in the kitchen and bathroom. If you can't sit on low chairs, how will you manage the john? You'll buy a laugh-inducing raised seat.

Surgery is never fun. And therapists are a pain in the neck, the arm, leg, hip, and back. Pick your joint. But, without them we'd be muddling around, doing our exercises all wrong, not only slowing down recovery, but causing additional injury. Ouch.

So let's hear it for the helpers. They might tell us more than we wanted to know about our not-so-fabulous bodies, but they get us back on our feet a lot faster than we could have done alone.

And they take all the abuse dished out by patients whose mantra is: "No thanks, I'd rather stay in bed."

It Ain't Like Home

In only a few going minutes the Museum of Decaying Kind can be attained. The hotel is in the Sutter Street and only two of block west far away from Union the Square.

So saith the description on my computer screen. In some bizarre way I had gotten an English translation of a German brochure on the hotel we had just kerbooked. At least, I think Einkaufsmogelichkeiten is German.

The glowing report failed to mention that Mickey the Grandfather lived under the bureau, but, what the heck. Chinatown was only six of block, and "in the lobby attached Cafe is served daily breakfast and the lunch." Furthermore belonged to the hotel cocktail bar named "Talk Room." If we got tired of chasing Mickey, my daughter Aimee and I could head downstairs.

San Francisco was really just a brief stopover. We had bigger plans: an Amtrak ride to Truckee, 6000 feet up in the Sierras. We would give daughter Martha a little rest by babysitting her nearly two-year-old twins.

After the usual hassles of a flight to the mainland, it was elegant to sit back in wide, lush seats. Imagine not having to share your elbow space with strangers. Not having to wonder if your personal gear was still under your feet, or if it had "shifted in flight." Oh, how I miss those trains.

Perhaps the first surprise was the litter. All sorts of objects were playing statue in the mud of low tide. Grotesque shapes turned into grocery carts that had been dumped down the side of the tracks. There were tires, bicycle wheels, even a truck bed.

A docent from the railroad museum in Sacramento was aboard to point out the highlights. Unfortunately, he had a knack for talking as the dining car manager broadcast his announcements, so you'd hear something like: "This is where the pioneers had to..." "First call for lunch...." "dismantle their wagons and lower them down the..." "four to a table...."

Approaching Sacramento, we realized how hot it was outside. A woman in her backyard was hunkered against the wall of her house, trying to squeeze into a square of shade. Her laundry baked limply on a nearby clothesline.

Endless farm country replaced the water; mile after mile of salad, with an occasional steak on the hoof grazing in a nearby lot. It was easy to spot the older farmhouses. They were huddled under a merciful island of shade trees, off in the middle of a field. Newer homes had young foliage, years away from shedding any comfort.

Farmers sliced their endless fields in tractors, seemingly oblivious to the merciless sun. The occasional creek bed looked like an alligator's back. On the bank of one pathetic stream, a little island of apparently homeless people was hidden in a tent, a baby stroller nearby.

Every town seemed to have its tag team. Even sewer outlets were marked in overblown letters. In the middle of a narrow squeeze of track, a wall spelled out Holden Caulfield's lament. The next rock proclaimed, "You suck."

Cubed hay was stacked by every roadside. Dead trees stood in the middle of stands, possible victims of lightning. The whole area was dry, dry, dry. Daughter Aimee, who spent several seasons as a fire fighter, called the trees "flash fuel." Since heat rises, they provide extremely dangerous tinder as fire shoots uphill towards homes. It was very sobering.

The one constant you don't expect on a train is the whistle. Always the whistle. Most of us have heard signals as we approach a crossing. But the train always seemed to be warning something or someone to be aware. Get out of the way. Wait. Hush; know you that I am God. Next night, a teenager was killed at a crossing in the area.

Slowly we changed grade and color, up to cooler land, where fir trees framed the skyline. Mountains wore snow caps. We were in ski country.

We actually passed under the lifts at Sugar Bowl. This would be a spectacular sight in winter. The train stopped at the small Truckee station. The babysitting was about to begin. The twins took one look at me and started crying. But that's another story.

Haleakala Times, September 3, 2002

Merry Christmas, DVD

How can it possibly take a month to hook up a DVD? It can't - unless the earth turns on its axis. Well, maybe that's putting it a little strongly, but surely there was something more than bad luck at work to make this Christmas present turn mean.

The first warning light came on when daughter Kathy said: "It's easy, Mom." Her recitation of which plug went into the DVD, the VCR, the television, the cable box, etc. was enough to bring me to my knees.

Some mutant gene allowed this child of mine to follow diagrams, just like in the illustration. She didn't realize that I thought DVD was men's underwear.

The fun began in earnest when I discovered that nothing could be plugged into the back of the old (very old) television set. I think Masa Hokama sold it when they were still serving lunch above his shop. RCA hadn't anticipated that anyone would keep the machine into the 21st Century.

Like the joke about buying a new piano to go with the piano scarf, I now had to buy a new television to go with the DVD. It was off to K-Mart, Costco, WalMart, Hokama's, Sears, Hamai, and anyone else who advertised. Meanwhile, I gave away the old set. (Is an alarm going off somewhere?)

Just before the three-day weekend, I picked out a new television. A husky young male struggled the carton into the front seat of the car. (Is another alarm going off? If I couldn't lift the box in the first place, how would I get it out of the car and up into the apartment? Slowly and painfully, with the help of a mover's dolly and a little stevedore language.)

Phase two involved connecting the three appliances to each other. This would be a merciful place to stop. The television set was child's play, compared to the tangle of wires behind the other two objects. Suffice it to say the long holiday weekend did not include watching the movie my daughter had thoughtfully provided.

Oh, well, at least I had the TV, except that the football players kept disappearing into the pulsing green blob on the bottom of the screen.

After the holiday, I called the 800 number in the manufacturer's destruction booklet, and a smiling voice informed me that something was burned into the picture tube. It could not be repaired. "Just bring the unit back to the store and get another one.

All you need is the original receipt and the original carton, with the barcode on the side."

Thank heaven for lazy housekeeping. The carton was still cluttering up the living room. The receipt? Oh, no! The day I bought the TV, I also picked up a video game for my grandson. It wasn't the one he wanted, so he had taken the original receipt back to the store. All I had was a copy, which some guardian angel had prompted. "No problem," said the customer service representative. "We'll give you a store credit, and you can pick out a new set."

Wrestling the 800 pound gorilla back into the car was not a chore to be undertaken lightly, but at least the end was in sight. Wrong. I had bought the last unit. "But it's on order." When would it be in?" "We don't know." Empty handed, I slunk home and caught up on crossword puzzles. No TV, no VCR, no DVD.

Next morning, challenging fate again, I picked out a brand that was in stock. The jinx held. I was stopped cold at the checkout line.

Somewhere, somehow, the credit slip had disappeared. The sale, which had already been rung up, had to be voided. What else could go wrong? The clerk's computer froze and someone higher up on the totem pole had to cancel the cancellation. Once again I had to leave empty handed, but not until after I had wheeled the hated object up to the Layaway department, and put down ten percent of the purchase price for them to hold the miserable thing.

Not all was lost. Some honest soul found the missing credit slip and turned it in, rather than spending it. So, next day I headed, one more time, to the store, only to be caught in a Kona downpour. Home again, still empty handed.

How do I like the new DVD? Don't ask.

Haleakala Times, February 18, 2003

Mother's Engagement Ring

Mother's engagement ring was won in a poker game. It was a wedding present from an uncle and came in the form of a pawn ticket. All Daddy had to do was pick up the jewelry. Uncle Phonse, a cigar-smoking judge, must have played in some high stakes games, because the diamond was the biggest I had ever seen outside of a museum.

Mother had the stone reset, to take some of the onus off the gift's origin. In those days, rings came in a velvet box labeled with a jeweler's name, not from a store with three balls hanging in front of the window.

Mother had other adventures, which set her apart from her four siblings. For one thing, they never seemed to leave St. Louis. Mother, on the other hand, moved to Havana after her marriage. My father's company, Fulton Iron Works, manufactured machinery to convert cane into sugar. They had offices all over the Caribbean. Unfortunately, her first pregnancy was misdiagnosed as a tumor, and she had to return to St. Louis for better medical care.

The adventures continued when my father was promoted to New York, where we kids were born. My aunts referred to Mother as "Poor Mary" because she had to live in the East. Mother, on the other hand, loved it. For one thing, she could smoke on the street in New York. Eventually, Daddy was transferred back to the home office in St. Louis and Mother's excitement went into mothballs.

It certainly disappeared when it came to matters of health. Every winter, we kids were lined up in the bathroom for our dose of Scott's Emulsion Cod Liver Oil, supposed to ward off colds. Today, the tonic comes in capsule form, but back then it was thick, evil-tasting liquid. The Life Saver candy did not make up for the vile taste. Come to think of it, that wasn't as bad as the dab of bitter aloes on the tongue, which was her punishment for being sassy. How do I know? Don't ask.

Sometimes, as a reward for "being good," we got to take Mother's ring out of the jewelry box and try it on. This was always a big thrill. The filigree setting incased all but the top of the stone.

We'd hold it up to the window and watch the colored lights flashing across the opposite wall. We couldn't understand why she only wore it on special occasions. In fact, there were times when she didn't wear it at all. Once, she spent six weeks in Mexico, where Daddy was overseeing the construction of a sugar mill. She was warned not to bring any good jewelry because of a theft problem at that time. ("They'll reach right into your car and grab your rings off your fingers!") So she bought costume jewelry, and swore that no one knew the difference. People tend to accept you at face value.

Mother always wore the ring on her weekly date with my father, who worked until noon on Saturday. She had the timing figured out to the minute, and walked to the curb in front of our house just as he pulled up in the car. They drove downtown for lunch in the dining room of a department store, and then to a movie. There were no multiplexes in those days, but you did see a double feature, a newsreel and coming attractions without any extraneous ads. Those were simpler times. My parents were always home in time for dinner. I don't recall them ever going out at night. We thought their lives were pretty boring, but then, in our eyes they were old people.

Mother died unexpectedly at age 52, and the ring was put away, along with huge chunks of our unfulfilled dreams. Eventually the ring was given by my younger brother to his fiancée. She wore it until their oldest son got engaged. It now graces the third generation of O'Neil women. Sometimes I wonder about its history. Who else wore that ring before my uncle won it in a poker game? Did anybody else have to replace it with costume jewelry for fear of theft?

Years later I had an epiphany about face value. While checking out groceries at Star Market, my own flashy ring caught the eye of a young clerk. She stared at it for a minute, and exclaimed, "Oooh, da ring!" I laughed and told her it was costume jewelry, bought at Liberty House for less than 10 dollars. She shook her head. "Not! Old lady like you wouldn't wear fake jewelry."

Mother, wherever you are, I can relate.

Haleakala Times, January 31, 2006

Play It Again, Mickey

The Seven Year Itch was scratched at last. We finally made it to Disneyland. I secretly hoped back in 1998 that grandson Kale might forget my rash promise to take him and a pal on the trip when he graduated from eighth grade. Hah. "Every time someone mentioned it, I counted how long I had to wait," he grinned.

Before we knew it, the party had grown to 10. The Disneyland Hotel turned out to be a serendipitous choice. The staff schlepped in cots, took our group pictures, and bent over backwards to make it the Happiest Place on Earth, as advertised.

We tried to cooperate. Except for extra towels and packets of coffee, we decided it would be prudent not to let the maids into our rooms until we left. Three generations cruising in and out of one suite could make it hazardous to a vacuum cleaner. There always seemed to be something on the floor: luggage, snacks, cousins.

With some of the kids and grandkids crammed into a hotel room during a family vacation to Disneyland.

Even the mishaps turned out all right. The second bedroom didn't have two beds, as promised, so we adults were treated to dinner at the Steak House restaurant. And boy, did we eat. And drink. When I ordered a martini, my daughters introduced

33

me to the gin in the blue bottle. "Mom, you haven't been using the best."

The older kids lived on Space Mountain, while the 4-year old twins stripped their parents' bank accounts for costumes and accessories. Every other child in the park seemed to be a pirate or a princess, barely able to walk in their oversized outfits. Old Walt's marketing genius was alive and well. I truly believe you could have bought a moon rock with a Mickey Mouse logo on it if you looked hard enough. Even the wall sconces in the hotel bathroom were held up by three-fingered, white-gloved mouse hands, er, paws.

Trash never seemed to hit the ground. Maybe that's an exaggeration, but it had to be one of the cleanest places in California. I missed the college kids who used to be such a presence. Wasn't that once considered the ultimate summer job? We did see a rather young looking Cruella deVille leading two terrified children down Main Street while their parents videotaped the event. And the daily parade oozed young Disney characters. But the people doing the sweeping seemed to be older ladies, for whom English was a second language.

Daughter Kathy and I tried to sneak in as much educational stuff as possible, so after leaving Anaheim we headed out in a rental car. After all, it isn't every day that Island kids get to see live polar bears, snakes, golden eagles, or the real Good Year blimp, tethered in a field. We stopped briefly at La Brea tar pits, where an excavation was in progress. The boys agreed "it was cool looking at all those cool bones," especially the ones trapped inside the tar.

Palm Springs was a disappointment. The fancy spa and casino turned out to be a spa on one block and a casino on another. When the temperature is 107 degrees, you aren't much for walking. Not surprisingly, we saw no flashing time-and-temperature signs. But there was an effort to hydrate the dry air. Water mist sprayed from awnings shading sidewalks where no one seemed to walk. Too hot. (To tell the truth, this is part sour grapes. We expected to spend money at the spa, but, as hotel guests, we thought we'd at least get to dip our toes in the healing spring waters. Wrong. Every single item had a price, up to Taking the Waters for $415. Kale and Lawaia didn't notice, because they had discovered girls at the outdoor pool.)

God did his part, however. Joshua Tree National Park was breathtaking. It had rained, so we saw some greenery, and the boys got to scamper up the biggest rocks they'll ever see.

On the way down to San Diego's zoo, we drove through a forest of 3,500 wind turbines, happily producing electricity for 250,000 of Southern California Edison's customers.

I don't know about the boys, but I learned a lot at the zoo. Jaguars are excellent swimmers and are known to hunt crocodiles in rivers. You can identify zebras by the stripes on their rear ends. Lions, being at the top of the food chain, don't have hunting worries. They sleep up to 20 hours a day. Dorcas means gazelle in Greek. A brown bear can consume up to 22,000 calories per day. And last but not least, giraffes use their 18- inch tongues to clean their faces and even their eyes.

There now. Aren't you glad you tuned in?

Haleakala Times

Queen of Lent

My mother was the Queen of Lent. Although she never forced us kids to follow her lead, our father's competitive genes always kicked in and we spent The Holy Season feeling inadequate. Even now, when Easter rolls around, I heave a sigh of relief because I no longer have to feel guilty.

No matter how creative we tried to be, there was no way we could outdo Mother. Everybody gave up candy. But she didn't stop there. She also gave up cigarettes. And the star in her crown? She gave up crossing her knees.

You laugh. Try it for just one day. Try it for half a day. It's such a natural position that we drift in and out of it unconsciously. Psychologists tell us that being aware of a gesture makes it harder to avoid. That, of course, fit our concept of Lent. It was supposed to be hard.

In those pre-Vatican II days, the emphasis was on "giving up" things. Ours was a self-centered religion. None of this modern business of doing something positive for someone else. We showed our spiritual stamina and earned brownie points by doing without something. And Mother was always the winner. God rest her soul, as the nuns would say.

Mother suffered through the Holy Season like a trouper, until Holy Saturday arrived and she began to unravel. Early in the morning she began the orchestration of her amazing pre-Easter performance. We kids wouldn't have missed it for the world. It started in the kitchen, where she cooked up a huge batch of fudge. This was cooled, cut into squares, and arranged lovingly on a real china dish. No melamine plate for this treat. The treasure was carried in procession to the living room, where it was placed on a table within easy reach of her favorite chair, along with a pack of matches and in direct sight of the clock.

Next to the fudge would be the cigarettes. A fresh pack waited in a clean ashtray. Mother had already torn off the opening strip of cellophane, peeled away the lead foil, and tamped the top two cigarettes partially free of the pack. There would be no wasted movements when the clock struck twelve.

All was in readiness. We kids had our miserable little bags of jelly beans, and my mother had her arsenal of self-gratification. Where to begin? This was not a problem. She had worked the system so she could give in to all three temptations at once.

With the first stroke of noon, she threw a piece of fudge into her mouth, struck a match, sucked smoke down to her toes, and crossed her knees. All seemingly at the same time. Ecstasy. All that deprivation. All those days and nights of saying "No" to her nature. Over with. Once again she had shown us kids that it was possible to overcome the weakness of the flesh. That you could stand up to Satan. Once more she had won.

Garrison Keillor says the Catholic Church in Lake Wobegon is named Our Lady of Perpetual Responsibility. He's pretty perceptive for a Lutheran. Or maybe he's heard of my mother, the Queen of Lent.

Second Time Around

Frank Sinatra sang that love was more comfortable the second time around. How about surgery? Is the second hip replacement any easier than the first?

After all, the basic drill is the same. They slice open the side of your hip, whack off the top of your thigh bone and drill a hole for the stem of the new joint. Then they ream out the old socket, replace it with a new one, and jam in the ball end of the stem. A few internal stitches and a dozen or so staples down the outside of your leg, and you're good to go. What's so complicated about that? It's when you wake up that the fun begins.

On the plus side, the second time around you know which foot leads the way when you're on a staircase. Like the catechism says, the good guy goes up and the bad goes down.

Another second-time improvement? You'll sew up the toe end of that hated elastic stocking so your foot doesn't stick out. And you'll break fewer fingernails forcing the thing over the plastic half-pipe that's supposed to get it up your leg.

I was determined to head off trouble at the pass by utilizing lessons learned last year, with the first surgery. This time before leaving Maui I had frozen home-cooked meals, cleaned the apartment, and scrubbed the refrigerator. The new iPod mini was loaded with songs to drown out the night nurses' debates about Ding Dongs vs. Twinkies. I was ready.

Daughter Kathy and I flew to Oahu loaded with walker, cane, elastic stockings, grabber, and chargers of the phone, radio, and iPod. The first self-induced mishap occurred at the Honolulu airport. We were so happy to find our suitcases that we forgot to wait for the walker.

Fortunately, Queen's Hospital has apartments for out-of-towners. Unfortunately, our room was right above the poker players gathered around the outside smoking table. But at least it was within walking distance of the admitting department, where I had to report at five next morning.

Some things were better. The surgeon didn't use morphine, so there was no hallucinating or Olympic quality gagging. Even more significant, the staph infection of unhappy memory didn't reappear. That meant no dreaded intravenous Vancomycin, no two months of upset stomach, and best of all, home in six days instead of eighteen days and fifteen pounds weaker.

Two seemingly small changes made a big difference. The first was dietary. With all the drugs competing for space in your digestive system, appetite can disappear. Of all things, salted hard boiled eggs suddenly tasted great. And for the times when nothing worked, little cheesy Goldfish and chilled Yoplait Nouriche breakfast smoothies were life savers.

The second innovation was the iPod. Instead of watching TV or surfing strange radio stations, with an iPod you can escape into Mozart, Hawaiian, Golden Oldies, or any of your favorites. This made a huge difference, especially in the middle of the night.

On the first day at home I walked into a chair leg and put the "good" foot temporarily out of commission. You do have to stay out of your own way. But thank God for all those pregnancies. Three of my daughters shopped, cooked, cleaned, decorated, and utterly spoiled me. When Aimee, the last to leave, ordered her cab for the airport, I momentarily panicked at the thought of being alone; this after twenty years of enjoying solitude.

Was the second time around better than the first? You bet. I was whacking people out of the way with my cane in no time. And there's a future benefit: with two fake hips, St. Peter will have no trouble finding me. All he'll have to do is point a magnet and all that metal will zap me right up... or down, as the case may be.

Shirley Temple Owes Me

Christmas season always reminds me that Shirley Temple owes me. Big time. I was at least partly responsible for her success, and she never even said "thank you".

It all started with an ad in the St. Louis Post Dispatch when I was a gangly kid. "Oh, Mama, look at this. They're giving free tap lessons at the Fox Theater. And the best kids get chosen for a show. Can I go? Please? Please?"

I had visions of being the Twinkle-Toes of Pershing Avenue; the envy of classmates; the idol of small boys. Talent? Inclination? Any previous interest in dancing? None of the above. But this was the age of Shirley Temple. Every mother in America wanted her daughter to have ringlets, dimples, and chubby little legs that could snap out complicated steps with Bill "Bojangles" Robinson.

And every little girl saw herself as a movie star, living on "the set", with a private trailer and her very own tutor. No more parochial school, with smelly boys whacking each other. California. Sunshine. Palm trees. Freddy Bartholomew. To a kid in the landlocked Midwest, it seemed like heaven.

Mother was more realistic. She knew who always spilled the milk; who fell up the steps; who rode her bike into a telephone pole. But this was the Depression area. Anything free was a bonus. Besides, she realized there was no way I could qualify for whatever scheme the Fox Theater was cooking up. She agreed, provided my older sister, Patsy, went along. And, icing on the cake, we could have lunch afterwards at the counter of Walgreens Drug Store. A real outing. I was ecstatic. Saturday arrived and we bundled up against the bitter St. Louis winter for the bus ride to fame and stardom. No doubt there would be a Hollywood director thanking his lucky stars that he had discovered the O'Neil Girls.

Reality slammed in as we entered the lobby. There, milling around nervously, were dozens of Shirley Temple Wannabes, all with---gulp---shiny, black patent leather tap shoes, tied over the instep with black grosgrain ribbon. They could make that staccato noise with their feet. We, on the other hand, were in our Buster Brown school shoes, with rubber heels, yet.

Outclassed in the lobby. God help us if we actually got on the stage.

As we advanced to the waiting area in the wings, we could hear the director calling out unintelligible instructions to the group up ahead of us.

"That's it. Turn. Double step. Shuffle off to Buffalo." We hadn't a clue what he was talking about. We looked at each other. I was all for leaving, but Patsy hissed: "Listen, you punk, you dragged me into this and we'll go through with it if it kills us. Preferably you."

In a trance, I found myself in a line of strange kids, all, it seemed, professional dancers. They were smiling, They were gesturing with their hands. They had a right foot and a left foot. I was paralyzed. Patsy jabbed me: "You're turning the wrong way."

A disaster. All those other little girls smirking in their tight little curls, with their short little skirts and their nasty little tap shoes. I hated them.

The director mercifully ended our misery. "You two. Thank you very much." We slunk off stage to the amusement of the next generation of starlets. I was near tears. Why had this ever seemed like a good idea?

We tried to make ourselves invisible as we shouldered our way into the frigid wind. No California. No palm trees. No swimming pool. No rubbing elbows with Mickey Rooney or Judy Garland. No Shirley Temple.

Shirley Temple? I hope she breaks a leg. There. I had said it. Shirley Temple inadvertently received the theater's traditional good luck wishes, because I was too dumb to know otherwise. So she owes me. Big time.

Haleakala Times, January 3, 2001

Shoulda Coulda Woulda

The things we wish we had done; or not done. Our memory banks are full of them, opportunities that somehow slipped by or that went awry.

Years ago I stood on a freezing London street corner and watched in fascination as sparks exploded off a charcoal brazier. A man was actually roasting chestnuts on an open fire. The aroma was tantalizing. Did I try some? No. There were so many "reasons". I didn't want to struggle with gloves. My feet were numb. I couldn't figure out the currency. To this day I can smell the chestnuts and hear the paper crinkle as he wrapped a packet for somebody else. And every Christmastime, Nat King Cole rubs my face in it.

On the same trip I had a chance to sample ostrich steak in Belgium. My hosts were teasing: "It tastes just like chicken." I weaseled out and ordered fish. Now I'll never know. Does ostrich really taste like chicken, or is that just the generic food joke?

Chances to stretch, to reach out. Why are we so afraid of them? We fuss when our kids won't try a new vegetable, yet we curl up in a negative ball at the thought of a change in routine. Dinner at nine? Oh, Lord, I'm asleep by then. A foreign movie? No, thanks.

Sometimes the opposite is true. The things we didn't say or do turn out to be the right choice. My older sister, who taught me so much, etched a painful portrait with this true story. As a young bride, living in a small midwestern town, she was far from home, family and old friends. Her husband, the newest attorney in his firm, got all the most inconvenient cases, out in the boondocks. He came home later and more exhausted every night.

One evening. as dinnertime came and went, her frustration threatened to boil over. When he finally dragged in, she held her tongue while her silent spouse toyed with his food, pushed his plate aside, and announced miserably: "I got fired today." Who knows what additional damage would have been done had she vented that frustration? My brother-in-law went on to become a successful attorney and a respected judge. But that night he considered himself a failure. And that night my sister learned to wait a little longer for the explanation.

With my sister Patsy and her husband Joe Stewart in St. Louis, where we all grew up.

Most of us try to be perceptive around those we love, but do we have even a clue about the needs of people who are another degree of separation removed? In his Hawaii Catholic Herald Column, "Looking Around", Jesuit Father William J. Byron relates a stunning experiment performed in a business school. A colleague of his included this question on the mid-term exam: "Please list the name of the person who cleans this classroom every day."

After the students' howls died down, the professor promised to include the same question on the final. He went on to warn them: "If you don't have enough sensitivity to recognize that a real person with a real name works for you every day by putting this place into good shape for class, then you're going to fail as a boss... by not noticing that you have real people with real dignity on your payroll who happen to be doing important but menial jobs."

Every human interaction, no matter how small, strengthens or weakens the chain. Did that man roasting chestnuts in London have cold hands and numb feet? Probably. Did I think of him as a real person with real dignity? To be truthful, I saw him as a quaint photo op; a Kodak moment. Too many degrees of separation. Another lost connection in the human continuum. Another shoulda-coulda-woulda.

How Honest Are You?

How honest are you? I mean, really honest? Sure, you wouldn't rob your kid's piggy bank. But what about the less obvious ways in which we all can be-- devious?

My own life of crime ended with abortive shoplifting in eighth grade. Or so I thought. Clean as a whistle since then. Or so I thought.

Then I remembered a sermon in St. Paul's Church, Grosse Pointe, MI. Now, Grosse Pointe has to be one of the wealthiest areas in the United States. All its statistics are skewed by the presence of families like the Fords (as in automobile.) This sermon had nothing to do with the Ford family, but there were plenty of parishioners who could have come close in assets. We were not among them.

The monsignor was talking about the commandment "Thou Shalt Not Steal." He made it clear that this was a pretty honest parish. Then he let the zinger fly. "I'm sure any of you could leave a fur coat on the communion railing all week, and it would still be there when you came back next Sunday. But do you pay your maid's Social Security?"

Fur coats I couldn't relate to. But Social Security? Ouch. We had a cleaning lady who came once a week. We paid her in cash, and hoped it wouldn't be ripped off by the thugs who waited for the cleaning ladies as they got off the bus in her neighborhood. This was shortly before the 1968 riots in Detroit, and things were heating up very uncomfortably.

Of course we didn't pay into her Social Security. Nobody paid into the Social Security of day workers. I'm sure the poor woman has long gone to her reward. But once in a while the nagging thought comes back to haunt me. What kind of life did she have when she couldn't work anymore? What kind of income did she live on? Or would subsist be the more accurate word? When you point a finger at someone, three more fingers point back at you. So I'm really asking myself: how honest are you?

Technology Strikes Again

Up to twelve hours! Set it ahead and go to sleep, serene in the knowledge that you will awaken to the heavenly scent of freshly baked bread, right in your own kitchen! The siren song of the Breadman literature called hypnotically.

And now those delightful sensations were to be mine again without the work. Without the mess. Just open the box of mix. Measure tepid water into the container. Add the dry ingredients. Spoon a cavity into the center. Sprinkle in the yeast. Set the timer and you're home free. Nirvana awaits. If I die tonight, they'll find me smiling.

I go to bed with pleasant memories of the process. When the children were little, I used to do this by hand. Measure. Knead. Drizzle in flour. Knead again. Shape. Then the rising in a slightly warmed oven, away from drafts (and curious fingers). It was such fun to open the oven door, carefully, surrounded by little Bottlings. Check the progress and inhale that magnificent aroma. Oh, my!

"Mom, the dinger went off. Is it time?" They can't wait. They'll eat a whole loaf fresh from the oven. Ease the treasure out. Carefully. Carefully. Admire the glorious, golden crust. Drive your senses wild with the enticing bouquet. It's as close to erotic as you can get in a kitchen full of kids in broad daylight.

Oven mitts on hands. Newspapers on the counter (a trick I learned from my mother. Cleanup involves throwing away the papers. Period.) Cake rack on top, for air circulation. Tap the pan upside down. Gently. Gently. The bread responds eagerly, gliding into place.

...Two o'clock in the morning... What's that sound? Ah, how wonderful. It's the paddles, starting to mix the dough. Back to sleep grinning as though I had won the sweepstakes without subscribing to a magazine.

Four o-clock, not really awake. Just turning over in bed. What's that smell? Be still, my heart. Herbs. Glorious herbs. Breakfast will be a royal affair.

Quarter to six. The machine clangs out an order: birth this ambrosia from its womb into its bassinet. Groggily I stumble to the kitchen, fumble with the light switch, and wince at the glare.

Raising the lid, I revel in the sensuous bouquet. Shall I eat a piece now, or be a good girl and wait for breakfast? Armed with hot pads, I lift the container from its cocoon. But where is it? Where's the bread? This shriveled, rock-like hunk of clay at the bottom of the cylinder? That's my bread? This cannot be. It smells so wonderful. It can't be ruined.

Well, maybe its salvageable. Ease out the fossil and at least have a taste.

Shake, rattle, bang. Stuck like a clam in its shell. It must have died in there. Rap on its side. Nothing works. Nothing will expel the wretched mess. I resort to violence. Ream that hunk of tin with a kitchen knife. Harder. Harder. Finally it slams onto the top of the stove, spraying hunks of crust into the burners. I forgot the newspapers. Bless me, Mother, for I have screwed up here.

Disgusted, I hack off one end. I am entitled to this much. Phhht. Spit it out before it poisons me. Nothing could taste this bad. Worse yet, the knife has damaged the lining of the pan, so it has to be replaced. Twenty-eight dollars. ("But Madam, that includes shipping.")

Later, after a couple of cups of steaming coffee, the light dawns. Dredging the box from the trash, I search for the expiration date of the yeast. Six months ago.

Hmmm. Let's see.... What time does McDonalds open?

The Long Way Home

It was my sister's eightieth birthday, and my daughter Aimee joined us in St. Louis for the celebration. Together we prowled the haunts of my youth. She had heard the tales. Now she could visit the sites.

She saw a trendy espresso bar. I remembered an old-fashioned drug store, and Mr. Dean reaching into a steaming cylinder of dry ice to retrieve a frozen Milky Way (five cents).

She saw the neighborhood library. I smelled musty pages of The Bobbsey Twins and Nancy Drew. Or was it The Five Little Peppers?

She saw a garage. I saw eighth graders leaning on the wall, puffing on cigarettes and talking about sex, concerning which we knew precious little.

She saw the building where Sisters of St. Joseph dragged us towards pious adolescence. I saw that innocence violated by a new, proud, terrible sign: This is a Drug Free, Gun Free School.

She saw the dime store. I saw my mother sobbing because I had stolen erasers to give to the nuns. (My older sister ratted.)

She saw the university. I recalled Jesuits in black cassocks, girls in sweaters and skirts and saddle shoes, guys I dated - or would have, if only they had asked. All still young.

She saw the residential hotel where my grandmother lived. I remembered a little old lady lowering a medicine bottle full of whiskey to a freezing rag picker on the ground.

She saw the family cemetery plot. My recollection was that of a fifteen-year-old girl shrink-wrapped in misery, catatonic at her mother's funeral.

She saw Tommy Wiener's house. I inhaled crocks of pungent, homemade dill pickles anchoring a kitchen corner. And shivered with the memory of a plump fowl being readied in the back yard for dinner. That's where we city kids learned the meaning of "running like a chicken with its head cut off."

She saw a manhole cover. I saw my brother on his belly, a long yard rake in hand, retrieving our one and only ball from the storm sewer.

She saw our old yard. I saw kids catching fireflies in glass jars on hot summer nights. And softball games, where my cousin Hilly had to bat left-handed because she was too good.

She saw our front door. I saw a Western Union boy delivering a telegram on Thanksgiving morning. The Secretary of the Navy regretted to inform us that my older brother, Eddie, would not be coming home from World War II.

We looked at the same things. But not really. She saw through the eyes of a thirty- something university art teacher. I was a child. And she just couldn't fit on my bicycle.

She saw a place. I saw a life.

Kihei Times, February 23, 1999

The Real Reason

Why do hundreds of people work thousands of hours to put on community fairs? Is it for art and orchids? Livestock? Quilts? Is it for the rides? The food? ! The underlying reason, the principal tradition that is honored every Autumn all over the world is this: to give young males a chance to troll for young females.

The whole thing is a big, outdoor mating cotillion, a gonad gavotte. The fragile, delicate set of moves was programmed eons ago into a guy named Adam. His youthful descendants are laying their vulnerability out there before God and everybody. Exposed? They might as well have had a skin peel.

Sure, they look cool. That's the whole idea. But the veneer covers stress levels squeezed up by testosterone. There isn't enough Right Guard or Left Guard in the universe for this tension.

They come in small groups, the guys; never a gang, and never alone. They move slowly in tight packs; baseball caps on backwards, young frames pumped up with jumbo tents that pass for trousers. The restless energy is palpable.

They're looking without seeming to be looking. At least, that's what they think. Every adult who ever went through this exquisite agony is secretly fifteen again, and aching for the boys.

Then THEY come into view, the subject, predicate and object of the evening. Gorgeous teenage girls; long, stunning hair, ankle-breaker platform shoes, "casual" outfits that took hours to pick out. "Does this top go with these pants? Does this make me look fat? No, tell me for real." A few wear as little as the law allows, and keep tugging at their clothes so as not to give away the store. They have yet to appreciate the art of concealment.

The pressure increases as girl pack approaches boy pack. "Here they come. Oh, God, she sees me. Oh, God." Turn the head a little bit the other way. Hands and feet suddenly too big to control. Nervous laughter erupts over nothing.

Females set the tone. WE will decide whether or not to acknowledge YOU. But inside their own heads, it's "What if he, like, ignores me? I'll die."

Girls' steps are choreographed just as precisely as boys'. Mother Eve knew how to maneuver her man. Most of the time, if the girls get that close, they're interested; maybe just Till-Something-Better-Comes-Along. But they won't bolt.

If the guys are lucky, some of them will be seen later as part of a couple. Their hands touch. He protectively carries her loot. A humongous stuffed animal is as good as jewelry at this stage. At least for tonight. At least while the Fair is in session.

Next Fall, who knows? They probably will have moved on to other relationships. But for this one evening, they are playing out the human condition in all its glory and all its anguish. It's their time at the Fair.

The Sleeping Porch

Did you ever wish you could wander through your childhood home and see what it looks like today? I just heard that the house where I grew up had been resold. I wonder if the new owners can hear our ghosts banging around?

It was a big old place, and we five kids slept on the third floor. As St. Louis summers steamed up, we knocked our clanking iron beds apart and dragged them to the cooler, enclosed porch a floor below. The little kids could manage a slat, and the middle kids could roll a squeaky head board down the stairs. But the uncovered metal springs and unwieldy mattresses required muscle. Moving, of necessity, became a community affair.

4628 Pershing Avenue, the home where I grew up in St. Louis. The sleeping porch, where we slept on hot summer nights, was in the back of the house.

In those post-Depression days, clothes were never discarded until the last child had outgrown them. So every school dance found a line of teenage boys trying on my brothers' jackets. Now it was payback time. Markers were called in, and our hefty male friends helped with the seasonal switch.

An air of excitement always accompanied the changing of the guard, both down in Summer and back up in Fall. By June, the flat roof of our house had turned the third floor into a sauna. It was time to clean the sleeping porch. The room extended over the entire width of the house, and three sides were windows. That's a lot of cleaning.

There was a comforting ritual to the process. Beds were reassembled, boys on one side, girls on the other. I was the tie-breaker, in the middle. When all was in place, we snapped sheets, fragrant with backyard sunshine, onto mattresses. No blankets were needed in that hot Midwestern climate.

The first few nights were restless. From isolated rooms removed from the rest of the family, we suddenly were a dormitory. Strange human sleeping noises assailed us. Predawn light woke us. And we weren't used to the creatures of the night, cats, dogs, birds, cars. Even the friendly Maryland Avenue streetcar, a Toonerville Trolly connecting line just a block away, was an intrusion. But, being kids, in no time it was Home.

The one thing we never could get used to was the parties given by the couple next door. He was a successful automobile dealer who liked to entertain. At night. He had converted an ash pit into a fancy soaking pool, complete with whooshing splashers. So the drinking and conversation carried right up into our porch. And that wasn't the worst of it. He had a slot machine in the garage, and sound effects included a flushing toilet. Secretly we kids were dying to see the slot machine and get invited to use the pool.

It came to a boil one night when my younger brother broke his arm. He was in a lot of pain, and couldn't get to sleep. The party was in high gear next door. Mother lost it. She phoned the "Next Doors," and gave them a piece of her Irish mind. I don't remember whether the party quieted down, but you can be darned sure we were never invited over after that.

Haleakala Times, February 4, 2003

Traveling Alone

"But Mom, you can't just go traipsing off through Europe on your own. You're an accident waiting to happen." My kids were heading home from Paris, and I was off to see Belgium, Switzerland, and who knew what else.

Never mind that I couldn't speak the languages, didn't know the money, and had only fifteen minutes to make the train connection in Brussels. Never mind that there had been no time at the station to buy Belgian francs; or that it was the dead of winter and I was still freezing in all the clothes that wouldn't fit in the bulging suitcase. My spirits soared. This was adventure!

In Brussels the first real scare. Up the escalator to track eighteen. No train. An attendant looked at the ticket, shook his head, and said: "No. No. Fifteen. Back down."

Were the best laid plans of mice and women about to go astray? Dry mouth set in. Half the allotted time had been used dragging that wretched suitcase up and down. Next trip it's two sets of reversible clothes, period.

Another shock at the foot of the gate. No escalator. Just two endless flights of stairs, at the top of which the conductor intoned: "No this train, you want...."

Desperate, I interrupted: "Does this go to Ghent?"

"Yes, but every stop. Forever getting there. You want number..."

"I'm taking this one." Another awkward push-pull down the aisle. Was it my imagination, or had this thing grown into a trunk? By now my goals had deteriorated to just breathing in and out. It got worse. When we arrived at Ghent, there was no sign of my host. I rolled the miserable luggage into the station, tired, hungry, and not a little bit scared. There was no Travelers' Aid station. No paging system. Everybody was speaking French. And I had no money.

The Visa card didn't work at the exchange booth. They didn't sell, they only changed cash of another country. I was directed to an ATM outside the station, across the street. Outside the station? My host said to meet him in the station. What if I left by one door and he came in another?

Would they at least let me make a phone call? No, they didn't have an outside line.

Think. Think. What's the worst that can happen? Well, for starters, you're an exhausted senior female tourist, traveling alone, with panic painted on your face, dragging a heavy suitcase, obviously lost and in trouble. Does that spell "easy mark"?

It was now or never. I sucked it up and went out of the station. What were Belgian francs worth in US dollars anyway? I had no idea, but punched the button for one thousand and got some funny looking paper back.

The money man exchanged a bill for coins so that I could use the pay phone. Make that "try" to use the pay phone. It swallowed the money - twice - and burped out a message in French. Since it was not, "Bonjour, Madame," God only knew what dialing sin I had committed. By now I was fighting panic.

One last hope. Two women at a booth were selling tickets to - what? I'd have bought anything at that point if they just spoke English. They pointed to a police substation, and there sat my savior. A young officer, fluent in several languages, had my host on the line in seconds.

It turned out that my daughter, who was worrying about my ability to use the phone, hadn't been able to complete the confusing call from one country to another. So my friend didn't know what time I was arriving. It all worked out fine, but if it hadn't been for a Belgian policeman who rode quarter horses in Colorado for a hobby, I might still be blubbering in the Ghent railroad station.

Waianapanapa, Here We Come

How long has it been since a bunch of Botts loaded the family car and spent a weekend at Waianapanapa? Twenty years? More? Well, get ready, Cabin Seven, we're coming again.

I have vivid memories of trips to Waianapanapa, that secluded state park on the outskirts of Hana. A black sand beach, hiking trails, sea caves, all were there for the trekking. Then there was the drive to Seven Pools, where we'd revel in the chance to play in the clear mountain water. (Unbeknownst to me, the boys would jump off the bridge. Auwe!)

The kids loved to go there whenever we could all get away. We'd make reservations months ahead of time, which gave us the added pleasure of anticipation. I'd cook up a pot of chili, fry some chicken, bring a couple of bottles of milk and some peanut butter and jelly sandwiches, and we were on the way. The last thing before we locked the door was to call the caretaker's office and ask Mrs. Oliviera if she needed anything from "the other side." She never did, but she appreciated being asked. Secretly, I think this had the added bonus of alerting the rambunctious boys that the caretaker knew who we were, and they'd better behave.

This upcoming visit, with only three adults and no rug rats - just me, daughter Sarah and her husband Kelly - will be a little more sedate. Once we unload the car, stow the food in the fridge, the pillows on the beds and the soap in the bathroom, it's Scrabble time. No television, no radio, no phone. Just us, and whoever rented the other 11 cabins.

Daughter Sarah is already on high vibe, reminiscing. "Mom, do you remember how sick I was that one trip?" Boy, do I ever. She wasn't the only one. A whole gaggle of us, including a mainland friend of daughter Martha's, had a cabin for the weekend. All went well for the first 24 hours. Then it fell apart. Sarah came down with some bug. Martha turned out to be allergic to the many mosquitoes, and was covered in welts. The girls were miserable. We had no option except to pack up and go home.

The drive was one I'll never forget. Sarah was curled up on the back seat, willing herself to die, whimpering, "Faster, Mom, can't you go faster?" Martha was clawing frantically at her bites. The final indignity? Her houseguest was car sick.

"Please slow down, Mrs. Bott, please!" But, as they say in the ads, "Wait! There's more!" To compound the felony, son Daniel's buddy talked nonstop. He always talked nonstop, but he wasn't always sitting next to me in a car full of miserable kids. Finally, in a frenzy of overload, I did what any loving mother would do.

I turned to him and screamed: "Shut up!" He did. For about three minutes.

It's a funny thing, memory. Martha has no recollection of the ride home, so vivid in my mind. But she does recall "feeling the presence of the royals" in the caves, on the beaches and paths around Waianapanapa. She remembers walking on black sand, the remnants of an ancient volcano. Such simple things we did together. But what far reaching memories they created.

Growing up on Maui, there is no short hop on the Metro to visit the Smithsonian's treasure troves. There are no Super Bowls, no Boston Pops, no Metropolitan Opera.

But our youngsters recall wondrous days of jumping off tournahauler tires on the beach at Keawakapu; of camping all weekend at Makena; of hiking in Haleakala Crater. They walked with spirits and visited heiaus in Wailuku and Hana. And, when they come back to visit, they want to do those things again. They want to re-experience what made Maui special when they were growing up. So that's why we're going to Waianapanapa - we need a "Maui fix."

Real Life 101

"Put down the gun -- please, Ma'am." His voice shakes. He is braced in the doorway, rigid with tension. Sweat gleams on his upper lip.

I sit warily at a table, pistol to my mouth. I want to kill myself. He wants to stop me. His partner, outside the door, bars my hysterical relatives from entering.

Desperate to end the stalemate, the two men whisper briefly, holster their weapons and walk into the room.

"Give us the gun, please, Ma'am."

I shoot them both.

This is not a perverted game of virtual cops and robbers. I'm a volunteer with the Maui County Police Department's Mock Crimes Training program, and these recruits have just flunked the Attempted Suicide scenario.

The Lieutenant is livid. "Gentlemen, take a seat," he snarls. He pauses. "Do you think you handled this well?" Pause. "Have you ever heard of officer safety?"

The rookies sit numbly while they are reamed by their supervisor. This blistering hurts more than the "bullets." But they are not alone. Two more teams will make the same mistake that night, and I will kill them all.

I am one of a group of people of all ages who work with the police department to hone the students' skills. In a few short weeks, if they pass, they will be on the street dealing with hysterical crime victims, strung-out drug abusers, and battered spouses. We give them a little seasoning, some Real Life 101.

Already these men and women have put in more than eleven hundred hours of training. They know how to fire a weapon and how to write a ticket. They are aware that an engine block gives more protection than a car door. They can find the knife in the sock and the gun in the bra. They have learned (they hope) how to stay alive.

But they have yet to experience "the public." That's us. For six or seven evenings we meet in the waning light at Lihikai Intermediate School, wolf down a takeout meal, and make life tough for the very people who could give us traffic citations in a short time. Under the watchful eyes of their trainers, we turn the school grounds into a hotbed of criminal activity. Sometimes the action gets so loud that real neighbors call the real police.

The evening starts with recruits' formation. We are secretly relieved to see the pistols being checked. No bullets, thank you. We aren't that eager. We receive our instructions from the training officers--the situation, the kind of resistance to put up. Whether or not to get abusive.

Fender benders and other less threatening scenarios come first, to give the nervous novices some practice at asking questions, writing in poor light, and spelling unfamiliar names, all the while keeping in radio contact with Dispatch.

Then we ratchet the pressure up playing stunned tourists whose car trunks have been popped at the beach. We become burglars hiding in a building. We mutate into angry tenants screaming invective at the landlord, who is screaming back. Usually working in pairs, the would-be officers learn how to control the situation, shifting us so we lose eye contact with our antagonists.

The strain increases as we go through domestic arguments, hit-and-run accidents, and disorderly conduct. By far the most demanding scripts are the drive-by shooting and the attempted suicide. These come last. (The latter can be so stressful that some actors opt out.)

In the drive-by shooting, the trainees are given a description of the automobile, and they know a weapon is involved. Real cars are used. It is the recruits' job to stop the car, locate the weapon and arrest all of us, without destroying the squad car's siren, public address system or other high tech equipment.

We offer resistance by refusing to stop, misinterpreting orders, protesting our innocence. They order us out of the vehicle one at a time.

"You! Driver! Put your hands out the window where I can see them. NOW!"

We are forced to walk backwards in the dark, hands over heads. We are spread-eagled on the ground, frisked, hands cuffed behind our backs, and hustled into the squad car. Handcuffs hurt. Patrol cars are not comfortable. As I said, this is not a game. (Try rising to a standing position with your hands tied behind you.)

If you've hidden the gun in your belt or a pocket, forget it. It's theirs in a flash. But a generously endowed woman has been known to get away with a small pistol tucked into the cleavage of a bra. If no female officer is present, a male is allowed to search for a weapon using a baton or the back of his hand.

During the course of the training, we cooperate or disobey, yell at, curse, and insult the rookies at the discretion of the supervisors. Actors are stretched, exhausted, sometimes bruised.

We want these bright-eyed neophytes to make their mistakes here, in the cocoon of a schoolyard, where the only cost is to their pride.

On the final night, there is a tremendous "high" when the troops line up and shout "Thank you, actors!" Despite the fatigue, the occasional lumps and the long hours, volunteers come back, usually twice a year, to take part in this program.

Does it guarantee us immunity from tickets when these eager beavers are out on the road? I wish! But I do know at least six young officers who will never knowingly step into a room where someone is holding a loaded gun. I know because I killed them one night in Mock Crimes Training.

Armistice Day

Eleventh hour, eleventh day, eleventh month. Armistice. Today we call it Veterans Day, and it covers all the wars--so far. World War I, the birth mother of Armistice Day, is generations removed from today's Nintendo Warriors. It was great-grandfathers in Sam Browne belts and puttees, Red Cross nurses and Morse code. And poppies.

No poppies blow in Makawao, between the crosses, row on row, that mark our dead. Poppy seeds sprout in soil rooted up and churned and torn, like it was in the fields of Flanders.

In the Ypres salient of Belgium, which was to have been Germany's pathway to France, Allied troops slogged their way to the Front in World War I. Belgian ground, bloodied through the centuries by men of Holland, France and Spain, would once again earn its nickname, "the Cockpit of Europe."

A Canadian surgeon, Lt. Col. John McCrae, spent seventeen days there in May of 1915. During that brief time he treated Canadian, British, Indian, French and German soldiers. And, in the absence of a chaplain, he buried one of his former students. Next day Lt. Col. McCrae poured out his frustration and grief in fifteen lines that continue to stab us today. Gazing at the nearby cemetery, whose ditches were filled with waving poppies, he wrote what has become one of the most recognizable poems from the War to End All Wars.

In Flanders Fields
By Lt. Col. John McCrae

In Flanders fields the poppies blow
Between the crosses, row on row,
That mark our place; and in the sky
The larks, still bravely singing, fly
Scarce heard amid the guns below.

We are the Dead. Short days ago
We lived, felt dawn, saw sunset glow,
Loved, and were loved, and now we lie
In Flanders fields.

Take up our quarrel with the foe:
To you from failing hand we throw

61

The torch; be yours to hold it high.
If ye break faith with us who die
We shall not sleep, though poppies grow
In Flanders fields.

We in America have not been touched by war to the extent that European countries have. In Belgium, there are sections where a visitor can hardly turn around without seeing white crosses in some sort of enclosure. The British alone have more than 150 cemeteries there. Battles on Belgian soil produced obscene numbers of casualties.

Tears still come at the Menin Arch Memorial in Ypres, where member of its Fire Brigade play "The Last Post" on silver bugles every night at eight, as they have for more than seventy years. No matter the weather, there always is someone in attendance as the tone reverberates. It is a devastating sound. And it isn't even for the Belgians.

This memorial was erected by the British to commemorate more than 57,000 of their 908,000 World War I casualties. It honors the ones whose resting places never were found; the missing. These were the men whose families were denied the painful closure of knowing where their loved ones lay; the dubious comfort of placing flowers, or rice, or whatever their culture demanded, on the graves of their fallen.

Colonel McCrae's student's name is one of those hewn into the eroding marble. They equal, within a thousand, the number on our Vietnam Wall. Another 34,000 are honored in Tyne Cot Cemetery, because they ran out of room at Menin. The death fields of Flanders are sanitized as being "rich in history." Make that blood.

Whether we call it Armistice Day or Veterans Day, tears continue to come in some homes. At Menin, Jerusalem, Serbia, Punchbowl, Arlington, they now have rest. But oh, at what a price.

Rob Me, Please

Does your body language say you're an easy mark? Do you mosey through shopping centers just begging to be ripped off? Frank Krau says you do. How does he know? "Crooks tell me. It's that simple." A private investigator who put in a long stint with Military Intelligence, Krau also worked for the state Attorney General. Today he lectures on the things crooks tell him. A big, rugged guy in jeans, he smiles like a choir boy but knows all the dirty tricks.

During a recent "Street Safe" talk at Kaiser Permanente, he strolled through the group and pointed out which purses he could easily grab and what women he'd avoid because "they're looking around; they're alert."

Here are some of the tips he shared, and the audience questions he answered. Shopping Centers? "You gotta remember, he's prepared. You're unprepared. He's been watching you. He wants your money, or something you have that he can sell."

How to protect yourself? "Start with body language. Be aware of your surroundings. Walk upright. Don't mope along with your purse dragging loosely from one hand. If you see the same man or group of kids going into every store you go into, find a security guard and tell him you're uncomfortable. Crooks don't like to be noticed."

Car alarms? "Who pays any attention? They're just an annoyance when they go off." How about those locking gizmos that look like big monkey wrenches? He laughed. "Thieves just cut the steering wheel in two and slip off the device. They can drive with half a wheel."

Walking? "Tuck your purse next to your body, preferably over your shoulder. Or use a fanny pack" He likes backpacks if they're worn properly. "But what do you see? They're slung loosely over one shoulder, because we're lazy." And carry a whistle. "You think I'm joking? What do you hear in a mall? Kids hollering to each other. Nobody would hear you yell. But a whistle? That's an attention grabber. Crooks don't like attention. "

Is there a safest time to shop? Absolutely-- in the mornings. "These guys on batu don't even get up till noon. They like the dark."

Parking? "Don't be ashamed to write down the location of your car. Thieves love to see people wandering around, distracted.

Have your keys in your hand as you leave the store. That way you can open the door in a hurry. And lock yourself in."

What things would make you look like an easy mark? "Wearing all the family jewels when you shop. They'll figure you're buying expensive stuff. And If you have to put parcels in the trunk, back the car up against the wall afterwards." Why? He had us slack-jawed explaining how easy it was to pop the trunk lid in seconds, using a couple of two-by-fours. "And it's not illegal to carry loose lumber in your truck." You should be backing into the stalls in the first place, he stressed. "Much safer." (This suggestion brought groans from the mostly mature audience of mostly females.)

Krau scolded the crowd for carrying too much "stuff". "You're going to the beach. Whaddya need? Your driver's license and ten bucks to buy the kids burgers."

Mace? "Right into the trade winds and back in your face. If you're determined to use a spray, practice by sniffing a little of it so you can see what it does."

Purses unattended in grocery carts? "Get stolen all the time. Maybe the guy just takes your wallet. You don't even know it till checkout time, and he's got a big lead by then."

The bottom line? "Trust your sixth sense." He related the story of a woman who moved from a bench at Ka'ahumanu Center because "something just wasn't right" about the man who sat down next to her. (He was carrying his rubber slippers in his hand.) The next wahine had her purse grabbed, and the barefoot thief was out of the mall, across the street, over the fence, and lost at MCC in seconds.

"The best weapon you have is between your ears. Use your brain." So, no more aimless schlepping around. From now on you can recognize us Street Safe attendees by our purposeful strides, tightly clutched purses, darting eyes, cheap clothes, and cheaper jewelry. If you're still not sure, look for the whistles. Thank you, Frank Krau. I think.

It Finally Happened

All the hands I've held, as an ER volunteer. All the bewildered families I've led to the conference room. All the ripped up, blown out, agonized, bleeding human beings I've registered, iced, comforted; all the calls for hotel rooms, cabs, chaplains. After the hundreds of Sundays, It finally happened. One of my own came in. A little eight-year-old towhead named Kale, with a left forearm grossly deformed, a victim of his own skateboard.

I leaned down and swallowed Kale in one glance. The tyke clearly was in agony, and frightened to death. Seeing me, his reserve crumpled. "Tutu, my arm hurts." God. I'd die for him, but I couldn't make the pain go away.

"Of course it does, Sweetheart. But we're going to fix it. Right now." The triage nurse asked if I knew how much he weighed. (He piped up: "Forty-two pounds.") She continued: Did he have any drug allergies? Was he on any medication? Who was his pediatrician? The triage nurse took a brief physical history from his dad. The information would influence the kind and amount of medication he would receive.

By now she had applied a temporary splint and rested the limb on a pillow, to stabilize it during the inevitable moving about. "Do you think you can stand up and let me weigh you?" she asked as gently as though it were her own child. To my surprise, he got up and walked over to the scale, where he clocked in at forty-nine pounds. "Why, Kale, you've gained seven pounds. Wait till we tell your Mom."

Wrong thing to say. Dads and Tutus are fine, but it's Mom they want when they're hurt. And Kathy didn't even know about the accident. The Men had gone to the skateboard ramp while Mom finished some chores at home. They weren't there five minutes when Kale landed on the heel of his left hand, snapping both bones in his forearm. A classic Colles fracture.

" When are they going to fix my arm, Tutu? Did I break it?" His eyes filled with tears again.

"You sure did, Sweetheart."

"Will they hurt me when they fix it?"

Ok, now the rubber meets the road. "Maybe a teeny pin prick." When the Trauma Room was vacated, the nurse wheeled the chair in and arranged the little form on the gurney. Moving around was jarring, but he took it bravely. I'm sure I would have thrown up by then.

65

"When are they going to fix my arm?" Again the plaintive cry.

"Sweetheart, they have to take some pictures first. But now the nurse is going to give you some medicine to help make the pain go away." She carefully rolled him onto his side, and he realized that, in this case, medicine meant shot.

Tears began to fall as he wailed: "I don't want a shot."

"Kale, you can yell or cry, but just don't move," warned the nurse."

He demurred: "I don't like shots."

"Nobody likes shots, Sweetheart. Anybody who tells you they like shots is lying." This seemed to calm him for a few seconds, during which time the nurse skillfully struck home. That did it.

"I want my Mommy," he cried. Boy, that will tear your heart out. Sick kids want moms. I swallowed hard and stroked his head.

Orders for X-rays had been sent via computer, and we all wheeled to the adjacent Radiology department. Kale was rapidly growing sleepy.

The X-Ray revealed one bone completely snapped, the other, at an obtuse angle, barely together; a green stick fracture. It looked terrible.

A call was put in to the orthopedic surgeon on duty that day.

"Tutu...?" Kale was getting blurry.

Leaning close, I asked him: "What, Honey?"

His face scrunched up for a few seconds, and he dopily mouthed: "I forget." Good. He was getting drowsy.

The arm was set and put into a temporary cast. A prepack of medication would get him through the next day or two. The real cast would be put on after the inevitable swelling had subsided. He wobbled out to the car, clutching his ice bag and his second set of stickers and fancy Band-Aids (for future use.) Now he could go home and surprise Mom.

When I called a few hours later, Mom related that Some Days it Never Ends. By the time they got home, Kale was breaking out in hives. Apparently he did have a drug allergy...to Demerol, the painkiller.

Next morning, when I called my daughter, she carried the phone to the couch, where Kale was watching tv.

"Guess what, Tutu?"
"What, Kale?"
"I broke my arm."

In Orbit?

Let's face it. You kept your parents in orbit for the first half of your life. (You know who you are.)

You were a rotten kid. But now you have a chance for the Big Atonement. Possibly you can redeem yourself.

What are we talking about here? A Texas-size idea. You, Sonny, can send your parents on a 240,000 mile funeral procession to the moon! Well, not all of them, just about seven ounces of their ashes. But think. Isn't that just the supreme act of filial piety? The ultimate lift? How much farther can you go?

What's that, you say, they're not dead yet? Of course not. You have to make reservations ahead of time. It's like life insurance. You have to buy it before you need it. Just think. You can guarantee that, when the time comes, your parents will Go Out In Style. None of this moldering in the ground, or feeding fish. No siree. Your folks will roar through space in a lipstick tube, along with 198 other cremains, to glorious peace on the moon. You, personally, will guarantee their spot on the lunar landscape.

How's that for atonement? Wouldn't that make up for a few peccadillos? Picture it. Your parents could fly into space on a commercial rocket from either Cape Canaveral or Vandenberg Air Force Base. They'll join Timothy Leary in the heavens. What's that, your Dad hated Timothy Leary? Well, tell him that Dr. Eugene Shoemaker, of the Shoemaker-Levy comet, made the trip. I mean, this is classy stuff.

For way less than the price of a luxury car, you can give Mom and Dad a glorious whoosh into perpetuity. A measly $12,500 puts you in the class of truly loving children.

Are there downsides? Well, yes. You can't visit their graves to bring flowers, rice, or paper computers for burning. There's no guarantee who will be in the next tube (maybe even someone of the wrong religious persuasion or sexual orientation?) You still have to dispose of the other five to seven pounds of ashes. And there isn't much room for an epitaph; something tasteful, like the heartfelt memorial in the small Presidio cemetery under the Golden Gate Bridge. One handmade marker reads "To my beloved rat Spike who made my life so much better."

How Average Are You?

"All the world art queer but thou and me; and sometimes even thou art a little queer." My grandmother used to lay that on us kids. She stole it from the Quakers, but it fits most of the human race.

So? Who's normal? And who decides who's normal? Ad agencies spend megabucks finding out who does what to whom, how often, when, where and why. They call it strategic planning, and it helps their marketing strategy.

Thus it is that strangers willingly answer questions posed by other strangers. We all like to be part of science. Bernice Kanner, a New Yorker who researches such things, gives us a peek at the nation's habits in a paperback, Are You Normal? It might not advance the cause of world peace, but it could help you win an argument.

For instance: who snores more? Six out of ten older men are guilty, according to the author. (Women start catching up after menopause.) What keeps us awake at night? Worrying about bills is Number One. Only two percent of us fret about natural disasters. But when it comes to real, knee-knocking fear, it's not the dentist. Hands down, it's making a speech in public.

About a third of us do our Christmas shopping all year round, but nearly a quarter of men, and nine percent of women, leave it until December 23 or 24. Lever Brothers research gives the lie to the ten-minute shower. The average, they say, is four. And the water temperature is 101 degrees. (That's Fahrenheit, not Celsius, in case any Canadians are listening.)

Only half of us eat Oreo cookies whole. And nearly half of dog owners allow their pets on the bed, despite the bouncing. Of the dogs.

More of us set our watches ahead five minutes than at real time. Nearly eighty percent of us don't make our beds every day. But half of us claim to change our towels after every shower. Most people change their bed linen weekly, but three percent of Americans at least say they change their sheets daily.

Men, you don't need to read this. The average bra size today is 36C, up from 34B a decade ago. (Manufacturers contend that over eighty percent of us are wearing the wrong size.) And nearly four percent of gals don't wear any underwear, the hussies.

Okay, guys, it's your turn to be embarrassed. Eighty-five percent of you don't use the slit in your jockeys. You go over it.

Fewer than ten percent of you have any idea whether you dress to the left or right. (Ask your tailor.) And you're not as big as you think you are (five to seven inches, not ten.) The average man spends 3,350 hours a year shaving his 5.5 inches of beard. And twenty-two percent of you have forgotten your wedding anniversary. Twice more men than women are guilty of this.

Who calls in sick the most? U.S. postal workers, according to the Bureau of Labor Statistics. More than half of us can use an ATM.

Only one in ten of us have had a professional massage, and only two percent of us have been bumped by an airline. An amazing twenty-eight percent of us have never flown. Of those who do fly, the preference is for window seats. Business travelers opt for the aisle.

What's the hardest thing in your life to control? Your weight, followed by your spending, fears and anger. Fewer than half of us have ever broken a bone, and the most frequent victim is the metatarsal, in the foot.

More than half of us admit to recycling gifts. The average American will move eleven times over a lifetime. And two out of five of us married our first love.

What's the biggest gripe? Telemarketers who call at mealtime, followed by childproof caps and newspaper ink. Junk mail? Two thirds of us ditch it unopened. The average family sends thirty-eight Christmas cards a year. What do married folks argue about? No, it's money, mothers-in-law, and which tv show to watch. And, final statistic, twenty-two percent of us--make that you--have rented a porn flick.

Selective Memory

Why do we have ice-clear memories of some things and almost no recollection of others? What triggers that freezing of a gesture, a look, an incident?

Thirty years later I could draw his face. It's that vivid in my mind. He was about four years old, a handsome little boy with a single, heartbreaker dimple. His mother was gripping him into the mall doorway of the store where I worked. She was frowning; chewing on some distasteful thought. He was oblivious to her mood, a little, warm blooded puppet. He caught my eye and smiled as though we were sharing a wonderful secret. I wanted to take him home.

His innocent charm was wasted on mama, who tightened her hold and dragged him off towards the linen department. As they left, he turned the sunshine on me once more. It made a memory that still feels good. Wherever you are, little boy, thanks. I hope mama has mellowed out a little.

*   *   *   *

I'll go to my grave feeling like a voyeur at the restaurant. The man and woman were impossible to ignore. Sitting at the next table, they were engaged in a painful pas de deux. His upper body was a languid adjective: aloof, indifferent. But the rest of him was a restless verb: a hand just a shade too long on her back; a touch just a little too high on her leg. They leaned away from each other, as though to deny the signals, all the while eating each other up with their eyes. I hope they resolved it. The tension was too palpable. I kept wondering which one was married.

*   *   *   *

The ride attendant at the amusement park was a big, gruff guy, bored with his job. He stuffed our coins automatically into his grungy apron pocket, not bothering to check them. And that was my hope. It was our eighth grade picnic and I was out of money, having spent the day's small allotment by ten in the morning. The only coin I had left was a twenty centavos Cuban piece, left over from one of my father's frequent trips. It was my good luck piece. Maybe, just maybe, I could pass it off. But then it would be gone forever. But it was so hot. And the day was so long. And it wasn't fun anymore.

Slipping the coin into his grimy paw, I hurried to the nearest Dodge-Em car and slunk down, paralyzed with guilt. It was not to be. A few seconds later he was at my side, grinning slyly and

71

announcing in a voice that shamed me forever: "You tried to give me your holy medal." Burning with embarrassment, I somehow found the exit. He might have failed as a numismatist, but I had failed as a criminal.

*   *   *   *

There were three of them, the boys flopped on their stomachs on the lawn. It was the last weekend before Labor Day; the last time off before school began. One of those gorgeous Autumn days, when the leaves were just thinking of turning. The trio caught my eye as I waited at a stop light. Bikes sprawled nearby, sneakers waving languidly in the air, heads close together, they were huddled in boydom. Serious idling time. I imagined their conversation: "Wonder who we'll get? Sure hope it isn't old crabby...." (You fill in the rest. Teacher? Boss? We've all been there.)

They'd be forty now, those nameless, faceless youngsters. I only saw them for a few seconds. But in the magic time it took the light to change, they were Tom and Huck and every kid who ever lay on his belly in the grass.

*   *   *   *

It was obscenely early in the morning. We were caterpillaring our way to the airline check-in desk. You could tell whose caffeine had kicked in. Certainly not his. He was just ahead of me and I sneaked a fascinated look every time the line turned a corner. The only part of his body that seemed alive was his feet. They shuffled on cue, never entirely leaving the floor. His face was frozen in neutral. He was, to all intents and purposes, asleep. How did he know when to advance? Was his radar so strong that he picked up the tiny puffs of stale air generated as the rest of us kicked our suitcases forward?

In a lifetime, how many people touch us, even momentarily? And how many strangers have sad, or funny, or happy vignettes that include us? We do, indeed, intertwine in others' lives, even if we don't know it at the time. Even if they never know it.

Kihei Has Been an Island Before

In case you hadn't noticed, 'tis the rainy season. The recent storm might have surpassed it, but in late January 1971, Maui was hit with the worst deluge in fifty years. It was so relentless and so vicious that people feared for their property and, in extreme cases, their lives. Don't sue my memory, but I recall it raining three straight days and nights.

When Jupiter Pluvius decides to visit the Islands, the old-timers count on certain givens. Kiawe trees will get their annual bath. There will be no dust for a few days. The intersection of Pu'unene and Kamehameha Avenue will be flooded. This storm, however, held a few surprises.

Upcountry citizens braced themselves for the freight train roar of trees fighting with wind, electric power and telephone lines. The police radio crackled with terse announcements of "Tree down, both lanes closed" or "Call MECO; wires sparking." Anxious fire personnel held their breath hoping they wouldn't be dealing with tragedy. Medics tightened (or loosened) their belts in anticipation of hairy ambulance rides. Big winter storms are a time of almost continual adrenaline flow.

The walls of our Kihei house, in which we had lived exactly one month, were literally dripping inside. The ground was saturated. There was no place for the water to go except down Haleakala to the ocean. It was a gamble, guessing which new ravine the flow would carve. To our family's horror, our house deflected the muddy water directly into the carport of our neighbors across the street. Auwe! How do you apologize for that?

The gushing continued down Ohukai Rd. tearing out great chunks of asphalt. Kenolio was flooded as you approached the old, old Kihei School, near where Medic One is now stationed. The grounds were calf deep in water. The intersection of Mokulele Hwy. and Kihei Rd. was a vicious river. A pickup truck could be seen off shore, washed away. Nothing moved. Except the water.

At the other end of Kihei the few condos were like islands of their own. The road had buckled south of the Hale Pau Hana, and was impassable. Kihei Kai Nani's swimming pool was one large mud bath. There was no beach at Kamaole II; just a three-foot drop onto rocks. Upcountry, a woman reported part of her roof blew off, and she was struck in the head by a falling frying pan.

It's not unusual for Maui to have several storms in the rainy season. During one such occurrence, radio station KNUI owner-manager Tom Elkins managed to stay on the air all night. There was no electricity, hence no lights and no way to broadcast. But somehow he dug up a portable generator, parked it in the yard outside his Ano St. studio, and was able to keep Mauians reasonably up to date. Ron Youngblood, Liz Janes and the other stalwarts called in descriptions of the havoc as they found working pay phones. There were no cellphones or digital cameras. This was the day of foot-slogging reporting.

Heavy rains had their ancillary effects. Sugar and pineapple plantations had to notify workers by radio if drenched fields would be idle next day. At the time, I was the "traffic girl" at station KMVI, logging commercials and other announcements to be read live on the air. At five o'clock one evening I answered a call from a man who was, to me, totally unintelligible. Three times I asked him to repeat himself. Finally he snapped: "How long you stay heah?" It was the point man from Hawaiian Commercial and Sugar Co., mumbling that "Due to wet field conditions the following shifts are not to report to work." I marked the messages for the very first thing next morning. But Cliff Arquette, the early man, picked that day to oversleep. The announcements were never made, and the affected field hands reported as usual. They had to be paid. HC&S was not happy.

So, this time of year Upcountry residents brag about how cold it is in their house. But you don't her them complaining that Kula Hardware is out of snow shovels.

Bill Me, Hotel Hana-Maui

I read where the Hotel Hana-Maui received yet another award of excellence from Conde Nast. It's always nice to see Hana get attention from the outside world. To those of us who live on "the other side" of the island, Hana is that delightful little town on the east end of Maui. We enjoy an occasional visit, but it might as well be on Mars. And I'm ashamed of that, because the Hotel Hana-Maui has been very good to me

For someone who's lived here since 1970, I've spent little time or money at the resort. If truth be told, I can only remember being there twice. And I'm sure the hotel would like to forget both experiences.

Back about 1970 my youngest son planned a hike through Haleakala Crater and out Kaupo Gap. After that he'd camp at Waianapanapa for a couple of nights and hitchhike back. This was in the days when anyone would pickup any kid and give him a safe ride home.

The rest of the family was watching television on a lazy Sunday afternoon in Kihei when the phone rang. It was the Hotel Hana-Maui. Some kind motorist had picked up my deathly ill son on the side of the road and driven him to the resort. Daniel had come down with a mean bug. The hotel welcomed him, pointed him to the nearest restroom, and took care of him until we could drive the infamous road to pick him up. He could not have graced their lobby as he lurched around, clutching his stomach. No charge. Thank you, Hotel Hana-Maui.

The second memory started out as a wild (for me) adventure at Waianapanapa State Park. My pal Eve Kiley and I were going to camp out, cook out, and be two self-sufficient single ladies for a weekend. She had a Volkswagen bus, which terrified me. When you sat in the front passenger seat you had the feeling that all the other drivers were aiming at you. Eve was a nuclear medical technologist at the hospital and smart as a whip. But neither of us was prepared for what happened.

The weather was't too promising, so we decided to claim our spot in the parking lot, get out the hibachi and have an early supper. An experienced camper, Eve had the essentials: cheese, crackers, and a cooler of wine. Oh, yes, also some food.

The area was beginning to fill up with others who, like us, had been unable to reserve cabins. We were smug and snug, munching our goodies, sipping wine and congratulating ourselves for being so smart and coming early. Dinner could wait.

Then it happened. The heavens opened. Hibachi fires drowned, children screamed, bodies flew into cars, and there we were, stuck. All thought of camping out vanished in the deluge. Hastily throwing things back in the van, we were drenched by the time our gear was secured,

I love Volkswagens. They have their place in the great scheme of things. But they never were intended to replace bedrooms. Eve's bus was equipped with something resembling a hammock, slung catty-corner between two hooks. She insisted that I "sleep" in that while she stretched her even longer frame--- where? Memory escapes me except to say it was one miserable night.

Next morning we awoke, or, more likely quit trying to sleep, and looked at each other. Ugh. Damp, wrinkled, forlorn and starving, we made a decision. The breakfast we packed couldn't be cooked. We would throw ourselves on the mercy of the Hana-Maui Hotel. So, bedraggled, unkempt, unwashed, miserable, we slunk to the dining room and asked if they could hide us at a corner table, way in the back somewhere. Nobody batted an eyelash. We were ushered in like queens. I don't remember what we ate, but it was served with aloha. Make that a capital A.

So, Hotel Hana-Maui, you've given me wonderful memories. And what have I given you? Sick people, wet people, and maybe twenty bucks? Not enough. I owe you, big time.

Good Move? Bad Move?

Some people live their whole lives in the same neighborhood. Not us. My husband and I pulled up stakes eight times in the first eleven years of our marriage. Most of these were company moves. He was transferred and off we went.

But one of the relocations was by choice. And that was the one with problems; the one that had me agonizing: what have I done? Because it was a child who paid.

At the time we were living on Long Island, N.Y. For a variety of reasons we didn't like the area. Good friends in nearby Connecticut urged us to join them. So the idea was incorporated into weekend drives.

To make a long story longer, we found a lovely, brand new home in New Canaan. It looked ideal. Country living with town amenities. Our friends were right. Good move.

Before transferring the children's school records, I went for a meeting with my son's kindergarten teacher at Flower Hill School in Huntington. She was a tiny thing with a little girl's soft voice. Not having time for a full-blown conference, she did the most amazing thing. She picked up a pint-sized toy xylophone and struck it gently with a little, padded hammer. In an instant the room full of tykes became silent. They responded to the tone as if it had come from an angel.

She explained that she wanted to talk to me for a few minutes, and would they please keep doing what they were doing and give her a little private time? Incredible. No rowdiness. Just a reflection of her own peaceful manner.

Then she said the words that would come back to haunt me. "Eric is an ideal kindergartner. He's equally happy playing with a group or sitting in a corner with his trucks. If you have any problems with him in the new school, it's the teacher's fault, not his."

Well, now. Wouldn't that warm the cockles of a mother's heart? So off we went to Connecticut.

On the first day I marched up to introduce my darling to his new teacher. She turned out to be a raspy, whiny woman surrounded by restless kids pushing and shoving. My heart sank.

We managed to speak for a few minutes, but as we were talking, a little girl kept trying to hand the teacher some flowers. In exasperation, this woman to whom I was entrusting my child turned and snapped: "Don't interrupt! Can't you see that I'm talking to this lady?"

Two weeks later I received a note: "Your son is disruptive in class."

The Screamers

It was the crying that did it. The two little boys sat directly behind me and sobbed most of the way across the Pacific. Why couldn't somebody do something?

I could empathize with the family. Years ago, when my husband was transferred, we flew from Detroit to New York with four children. The baby, Sarah, fussed all the way to the airport, then fell asleep just as we got out of the car. Again, she fussed throughout the plane ride, dozing off as we landed.

Even without the noise, this recent fight was no bargain. The single, narrow aisle was usually crowded with attendants hawking drinks or headsets, or pushing metal carts. It was like a monster obedience class where everyone had been ordered to: "SIT" The few times it was empty of crew, the aisle quickly filled with passengers trying to get to the restrooms or just stretching their cramped legs. When you added the crying, the skies became-- what's the opposite of friendly?

The little ones sounded so miserable. They rigidly refused to be comforted. Were they hungry? Why didn't the parents feed them? Were they wet? Sick? Change them. Give them some medicine. For heaven's sake, Do Something!

Later in the trip I learned the facts. These were foster parents, and the youngsters they were desperately trying to soothe had brain damage from severe abuse as infants. Throwaway kids in a temporary shelter, the babies didn't cope well with changes in their environment or routine.

Suddenly I felt ashamed. This couple was doing a job most of us could not, or would not, undertake. And I was annoyed because these tiny victims were disturbing us fat cats?

Why hadn't somebody offered to take one of the boys for a few minutes? Just hold him. Or stroke him. Walk with him. Talk to him. Would it have killed one of us to give these exhausted foster-parents a brief respite? Why didn't someone offer to help? Yeah. Why didn't somebody?

Why didn't I?

Disneyland Interrupted

The four of us were just buckling up for the flight to California when the announcement came over the intercom. Capt. Mimi Tomkins would be our pilot. Daughter Kathy and I exchanged dropped jaws. Fourteen-year-old grandson Kale and his pal Lawaiah were unimpressed. They were quivering with excitement about the upcoming family reunion at Disneyland. But Kathy and I were jolted back 17 years to Maui Memorial Medical Center. It was chicken skin deja vu.

That fateful day Capt. Tomkins had been co-pilot aboard Aloha Flight 243, which made a spectacular emergency landing on Maui after losing much of its fuselage. Airplane inspection standards would change that day. And Kathy and I would meet more than once at the hospital, where I manned telephones and ran errands as an ER volunteer. She had a much more hands-on job. Down in the trenches with medic partner Dennis "Fitz" Fitzpatrick, she treated and transported victims from the plane to the hospital.

When the pilot found out that a paramedic from "the incident" was on board, she sent word that she'd like to meet in the cockpit after landing. Neither she nor my daughter had had any contact with "the other half", Kathy with the flight crew, Capt. Tomkins with rescue personnel. They had a lot to talk about.

I was surprised to find a friendly ("Call me Mimi"), petite, fair-haired woman who looked like she might just have graduated from college. She and Kathy exchanged war stories as we walked to the terminal, each supplying details unknown to the other.

Mimi explained that, from where she sat, she couldn't tell what had happened. After a loud noise, communication with the cabin was lost. "Each pilot could see a different part of the tail. That was it." Debris was floating in the cockpit; the entry door was missing, and there was blue sky where the first class ceiling had been. But neither officer was aware of injuries; certainly not the disappearance of the senior flight attendant who was on her last run before retiring, and who apparently was sucked out of the plane.

Of the 95 souls on board, there were eight serious injuries and 57 classified as minor. The $5 million plane was dismantled and sold for scrap. Having lived through the scare, Tomkins later became active in a stress debriefing program for crew members.

She was interested in hearing details of the work done on the ground that day by local teams. Every Maui ambulance had been called in. Every physician who could get there showed up at the hospital. It was a massive, unscripted performance.

Kathy described being in Medic Two's station on Makawao Ave., blissfully unaware of the event until the phone rang. The emergency 9-1-1 radio channel was so busy that it took a landline call to activate the upcountry paramedics.

"We thought a plane had gone down," she explained. "Nobody really knew what had happened. We were the second ambulance to arrive. Medics at the scene were triaging patients, determining who should be transported first. You couldn't tell whether blood on a victim was theirs or somebody else's. There were lots of cuts and eye injuries from wind and flying debris."

Mimi was eager for details new to her. "We transported seven people on that run," remembered Kathy. "A flight attendant with a broken arm sat up front with me. Fitz had his hands full in back with two patients on stretchers and four on the floor, including a Japanese woman with a skull fracture and a man with burns. I was driving and at the same time trying to comfort my patient. She was in a lot of pain. Finally I thought of a way to relax her, and I said, 'you know, you really ought to do something about your hair. There'll be a lot of people at the hospital.' A true female, that gal brought her good arm up to the mess of debris on top of her head and broke out laughing. It worked. Fitz couldn't figure out what was going on."

A postscript. After returning from Disneyland (yes, we made it. More on that later.) I asked Fitz about his recollections. He said Kathy phoned him excitedly the next morning. "Turn on the television. We're on Good Morning America."

He remembers telling her: "Yeah? Well, I was leaning over a passenger, and the camera didn't catch anything but my butt. Only my mother would recognize me."

A few minutes later he got a call from his mother. "Honey, I saw you on tv!"

Thanksgiving Memories

We thought the chaplain's office was sending us a nice Catholic farm girl from Des Moines. Who showed up? A nice Mohammedan boy from Egypt.

No matter. It turned out to be one of our most memorable Thanksgivings.

Living in a Connecticut suburb, we sometimes felt like Wonder Bread sandwiches stuffed with clones. So my husband and I went out of our way to expose the kids to people from different backgrounds and cultures.

How? For starters, the nearest university always had students who couldn't go home for the holidays.

Enter Ali Ahmed. Hardly a "college kid," he already held a degree from the University of Cairo, and was working on his doctorate at Columbia.

He lived in a Manhattan apartment filled with Russians who had earlier fled their homeland. A bachelor, we wondered how he would react to seven kids, ranging from twelve down to two years.

Fabulously. Ali, a classic extrovert, reveled in his role as a teacher. Our eldest son, Brian, was studying Egypt in preparation for a class visit to the United Nations the following week. He learned more from our guest than he did on the trip. Egyptian kings? Which dynasty? Mummies? What social class?

Oh, there were a few glitches. I had prepared the traditional Thanksgiving turkey dinner. Our guest was a strict vegetarian. And we weren't expecting the phone call from Brian's study pal: "What time should I come over and what should I wear and can I bring my Dad?"

Ali loved it. The more the merrier. As he proclaimed, "I'm the best Egyptian cook in New York. Next time I'll bring the food and make dinner."

He never did make dinner, but he did come back to prepare baklava, which the older children took to school next day to share with classmates.

Not all our visitors were college students. There were three Swedish businessmen who wanted to see an American family at home. Trying to be perfect hosts, we bought a bottle of Aquavit, said to be their national drink. They broke the seal on the bottle but decided they'd rather have martinis.

And where do you place Mrs. Vas, "the passport lady"? An upper class Hindu from Bangalore, she spent a weekend with us when we lived near Detroit. A childless widow resplendent in flowing sari and elegant jewels, she won the children's undying love by playing games with them.

But she didn't seem to realize that, unlike her own home in India, this one had no maid. Or so she pretended. Secretly I wondered if I was being snookered.

Oh, yes, the passport. The one thing Mrs. Vas wanted to do was drive across the Detroit River to Canada. This was no problem for us, but she was not an American citizen. There were several tense moments regarding a visa, and I had some ungracious thoughts about the possibility of a permanent guest who was used to servants.

Visitors enriched our lives. We learned geography, history, and plain humanity as we shared meals with "foreigners." Yes, it was extra work. And yes, there were awkward moments. But that's not what we remember.

Even today my kids reminisce about the people they met around our dinner table. Hopefully it was a two way street. I like to think our guests took a bit of our country home with them.

And Mrs. Vas? Surely she realized that not all American women had small families and cooked only canned goods.

Once Upon A Time

My kids used to shiver in delight when I pointed to the ogre's picture and roared: "I smell boy!" They already knew Jack would slide safely down the beanstalk. No matter; the anticipation was delicious. And the memory is still fresh in my mind, though they are grown and have children of their own.

So I was a bit surprised at the reaction of daughter Kathy when I gave her a birthday present of my very dog-eared copy of "Once Upon A Time, A Book of Old Time Fairy Tales". It had been a birthday present to me when I was just learning to read. I thought she would glance at it, then stick it away someplace. On the contrary, she handled it like a relic. Devouring the fragile pages, which were slipping away from the string binding, she was lost in "I remember."

It wasn't long before she found a more recent edition on the internet, and I ordered two copies for old time's sake. The first arrived Christmas Eve, along with children and grandchildren here for the holidays. This new version was smaller, but had the same wonderful illustrations by Margaret Evans Price. The heroines were still achingly beautiful, the heroes devastatingly handsome, and the villains equally loathsome. I was six years old again, in wonderland.

Christmas morning I brought the new book to the family gathering and gave it to daughter Martha for her four-year-old twins. This would make the third generation of my family to fall in love with this special volume.

In the midst of the morning chaos, little Montana and I snuggled on the sofa to look at the pictures. She wanted to know why there was a wolf in Grandma's bed. I was transported back forty years when my kids squeezed together, listening to the same stories, asking the same questions.

Perhaps the biggest surprise came when the young teen girls heard us reading. Forget about the new earrings. Put the clothes back in the boxes. They were fascinated by stories they, too, knew as toddlers. Hop O' My Thumb again pulled off the ogre's boots. Drakestail once more waddled up the leaning ladder.

Not every story is there My six-foot son Eric was disappointed that Jack the Giant Killer was missing. No more frightening bellow of "Fe, fi, fu, fum. I smell the blood of an Englishman." But there was more than enough to delight anyone old enough (or young enough) to enjoy a return to fantasyland. The magic is still there. As Katherine Bates says in her introduction to the original edition: "It is a pity, but there are people who say fairy tales are not true."

What a shame.

The Last Flight Home

Never take the last flight home. Never. You're asking for trouble.

The idea sounded enticing. Why rush to Oahu for an early morning meeting, and rush back to Maui? Book the last flight and hang around Honolulu for a while. Roam through Ala Moana Shopping Center. See what the city folk are up to. Enjoy a leisurely dinner in a new restaurant.

Everything worked like a charm until I came home. Maui was in the grip of a torrential rainstorm. This was in the days when you exited the plane from the tail section, and walked across the tarmac to the terminal.

Sloshing to the car, I sank into the dry seat and sighed with relief. In half an hour I'd be home. Not quite. The battery was dead. It was the eve of a holiday. Tow trucks were answering other calls. The airport was shutting down. My options were reduced to one: rent a car.

There was still one agency open, and fortunately they still had a car left. One car. Unfortunately it turned out to be a Super Belchfire Eight, king size luxury model, loaded with extras I couldn't begin to operate, and didn't need in the first place. But I was stuck. The rental agent was equally anxious to get home. He handed me a contract and the keys to The Car From Hell.

Ominously, the seat refused to come forward. The last driver must have been a basketball player. Well, maybe if I sat up real high....Turning the ignition key activated every option. The dashboard blasted cold air. The radio shrieked rock and roll. The windshield wipers were stuck on super fast. No matter how many knobs I twisted, the assaults continued. At least there was no danger of falling asleep on the drive to Makawao.

Finally the ordeal came to an end. I crawled into bed, exhausted. Thank heaven it was all behind me.

Next morning I headed to the carport, and there stood...nothing. The car had disappeared. Had I dreamed the whole thing? Nothing so esoteric. Apparently I had neglected to set the parking brake. During the night, the neighbors' cats must have have chased each other all over the vehicle enough to nudge it down a slight incline. And there it leered drunkenly atop some bushes, its trunk mooning me in a final act of defiance.

Try explaining that to the tow truck driver and rental agent. As I say, never take the last flight home.

It Could Be You

This is for the Maui High students who dissed Barbara Babb when she tried to talk to them about drinking and driving. (The Maui News, Oct. 12.)

Not to worry. The medics will scoop you up and strap you into an ambulance. You might gag as they try to get a breathing tube up your nose. They might break a rib or two as they fight to pump your heart into beating. Relax. You won't feel a thing.

Your parents and friends? Now that's a different story. Because it's too grisly for them to watch you being shocked, they will be grieving out in the hospital lobby in front of total strangers, or secluded in a conference room. There might even be a police chaplain there who will try to soften the blow.

They have to pronounce you dead? Nothing worked? The ER staff hates it when that happens. But you won't feel a thing. Your parents might tear the air with screams of "No! No!" but don't feel bad. You won't hear it.

By the first anniversary of your death, your honey probably will be dating someone else. Your sibs will have trouble concentrating in school. They keep remembering you in a casket; the first dead person they ever saw. Your parents will be depressed. They'll keep blaming themselves. They'll go to their own graves torn in two, because parents aren't programmed to lose their kids.

But, hey. Not to worry. You'll probably be floating around somewhere, wishing to God you had a second chance to come back and do it differently. Or at least to tell the kids at Maui High: Listen up. It CAN happen to you. Don't drink and drive.

Emily Bott
Emergency Room Volunteer

Letter to the Editor, Maui News, Oct 24, 1998

Anchors Aweigh!
Wild Women on Around-the-Islands Cruise

By the time you read this, we'll be somewhere between Kahului and Nawiliwili, on the Pride of Aloha. My friend Les and I already have a lot of happy nonsense under our belts, so this should be fun.

Twenty some years ago I took a solitary trip around the islands on the Oceanic Independence. Or was it the Constitution? Memory fails. But I know it was nicknamed the Indigestion or the Constipation, so I'm packing both kinds of meds.

It will be interesting to see what has changed. Some of the differences are already apparent. For one thing, we can board in Kahului. On the first trip, passengers had to fly to Honolulu. The whole experience was more festive then. Friends and relatives crammed the stateroom laden with lei and champagne for a bon voyage party. I had the steward arrange for canapes. Since 9-11 (aren't you getting to hate that phrase?) outsiders are not allowed near the dock, much less on the ship. So we ladies will schlep our suitcases to the gangplank, where younger, stronger hands will roll them to the stateroom. We hope.

An internet search turned up reviews by former passengers, who gave both bouquets and brickbats. The articles were two years old, so we're practicing positive thinking. Surely the negatives have been taken care of by now. To be on the safe side, we're packing sweaters and planning to get to the food before the day trippers return from their helicopter rides, or golf games, or snorkeling excursions. We've both been there, done that, so this is an eating, sleeping, hot tub excursion.

We might get off long enough to visit the chocolate factory in Kauai or Kailua-Kona. We hear there's another one in Hilo. And we've promised each other to stay awake long enough to experience the ship's nighttime passage by spectacular Kilauea.

Another thing we're planning (don't tell anybody) is smuggling our own wine aboard. Norwegian Cruise Lines frowns on this. Meals are included in the price of the ticket, so they expect to make a profit on the spirits. They charge a corkage fee, said to be $15, on anything you bring aboard. If they catch you. Stay tuned.

For those who remain on the ship, what's to do? I'm looking at the glossy magazine they give you ahead of time. It promises a week of obscene luxury. Our stateroom has a television set, refrigerator (to keep our wine chilled), and a safe. Les can have

Wild women at Aloha Tower. Les Gibson and the author on a shore break during a cruise of the islands.

the safe. I learned long ago not to bring good jewelry on a trip. Just wear something you can afford to lose, and your kids can identify in the case of an accident. If we get hungry for more than Maui chips, there are six restaurants and thirteen bars and lounges. The dining areas feature open seating. This is a distinct improvement over the first cruise, where I was assigned a place next to an elderly gentleman who either couldn't, or wouldn't, talk. Those were long meals.

Strangely, this entire expedition is the result of a mistake. It was originally promoted as a group outing by the Red Hat ladies, those wild women over fifty who have so much fun. We signed up immediately. It went downhill from there. Unbeknownst to us, the dates didn't work out for the Hatters, and the official trip was postponed. So we may well be the only wild women aboard.

I don't know about Ms. Gibson, but I don't plan to spend much time around the basketball court, the golf driving nets or the video arcade. But the walking track should be a lot more interesting than the hall of my apartment building. Imagine doing your laps with the clear ocean breeze in your face, rather than guessing which neighbor is cooking fish for dinner.

We briefly considered booking the "owner's suite", complete with a hot tub on the private balcony, a living room, bar, separate dining area, butler and concierge. But it's so big that we'd probably get lost.

And the difference in price will buy a lot of chocolates.

Haleakala Times, Oct. 11-24, 2006

Les Gets Busted

Back on dry land! In the last chapter, Les and I were trying to save money by smuggling booze aboard the Pride of Aloha. My cheap wine sailed through, undetected. But X-ray screeners "weren't quite sure what an object was" in my friend's suitcase. She had to open it in the Security office. Les had been busted. And it wasn't even her idea in the first place. The young man watched politely as she zeroed in on a tiny, sample serving of Maui Ocean Vodka. He didn't ask about the other five bottles, and we didn't volunteer.

If that was the low point of the seven-day trip, then passing within a mile of Kilauea volcano at night surely was the high point. The captain slowly steered a full circle to guarantee clear views for passengers on both sides of the ship. Mauna Loa seemed alive with embers. There were some monster-size cameras recording the spectacle, which reminded us of our impotence in the face of nature's power. And this was before the earthquake!

During the daytime, most passengers disappeared on shore excursions, so we pretty much had the place to ourselves. We luxuriated in the on-board amenities: pool, hot tub, library, theater, shops, internet cafe. We docked in Honolulu, Nawiliwili, Hilo and Kona before returning to Kahului.

Kauai's vans sported the most unusual signs: "See Kauai through Hollywood's Eyes"; "Kauai ATV-Do Something Dirty." Honolulu had the Aloha Tower Market Place, which is a lot of fun. The ship seemed so big that we were lost half the time. Early on, we abandoned the goal of walking the track every morning. We put on more miles just trying to find our way around.

We enjoyed watching the Cruise Director lead trivia contests and general nonsense by the outdoor swimming pool. An elderly man won a "Knobbiest Knees" sash and refused to take it off, to the chagrin of his wife.

A few yards past the pool was the outstanding feature of Deck Eleven, the buffet. It was probably the only place we had no trouble locating. Food became a quest. We tried one of the four fancier restaurants, but why wait for a sit-down dinner in a room full of old men in tuxedos when you can gawk at 300 pounds of food? And that was just on the plates of fellow passengers. We feasted on salmon steaks, prime rib, swordfish, leg of lamb, chicken, roast pork, and pasta. In a salute to our island home, they featured

Kona coffee, C & H sugar, and, the most popular dish on the menu, Roselani Ice Cream.

At first we thought all those people in white uniforms had gone through the Merchant Marine Academy. Mistake. The ones with wide gold bands on their shoulder boards were employees of Norwegian Cruise Lines. Speaking of the crew, they were extremely friendly. As my roomie said: "There are eight hundred of them, and every one has said 'Aloha' to us at least once." The other phrase we heard frequently was "in the unlikely event of an emergency."

There were no emergencies while we were aboard, as far as we knew. "In the unlikely event," there was a fully staffed sick bay. For a while we wondered if there was a flu epidemic going on, because the restaurant areas suddenly seemed awash in globes dispensing alcohol as you held your hands under them. Smiling crew members "suggested" that you avail yourselves of this sanitizing measure.

All in all, we had a blast. If you're planning a similar trip, here are some things we learned. Make a little personal map of the ship. The signage isn't that great, and there are at least three different sets of elevators. Bring a sweater and comfortable shoes. If you forget something, the shops are fully stocked, including the triangular case that holds a folded American flag. I was tempted to ask if they planned a burial at sea.

Oh, yes. If you're thinking of smuggling your own wine aboard, you have a fifty-fifty chance of success.

Haleakala Times, Nov. 8, 2006

Flying First Class?

Normally I'm in the boarding line that hunkers against the wall, watching the rich folks claim their seats. But on occasion I, too, have traveled First Class. Is it different? You bet your booties. Here are two travel stories. One was sad, the other? You be the judge.

The first flight, a 10,000 mile round trip between Kahului and St. Louis, took place last month. I don't sleep well on planes, and won't take the all-nighter unless it's an emergency. This qualified. A beloved young nephew had died unexpectedly and I grabbed whatever reservation was available, with one caveat. It had to be First Class. There would be enough stress without risking a miserable seat assignment.

You might as well be on a different plane when you fly First Class. Unlike Coach, where you get no beverages until the "fasten seat belt" signs disappears, we were offered libations as soon as we stepped aboard. "Would you like something to drink" was practically a mantra. You can slug down a nightcap while still on the ground. They even apologize as they remove your glass for takeoff. "I'll bring you another one as soon as we're airborne."

Depending on the meal, you might get real silverware and real cloth napkins. You'll also be offered scalding finger towels, which you might drop. Sleeping is at least theoretically possible in First Class. The cabin is quieter, and the seats, which are much wider, recline without whacking the person behind you.

But even paying extra can't guarantee scheduling. The nine p.m. flight landed in Salt Lake City at six in the morning local time. This was two o'clock body time, and I had been awake since two-thirty the morning before. Say "sleep-deprived." The next leg, to St. Louis, wasn't scheduled to leave for more than three hours. That's a lot of "walking around" time. Last minute reservations aren't necessarily the most convenient.

Salt Lake City jetways weren't covered, like the ones on Maui. The terminal building was only one story high, so we had to walk out into the bitter cold and up a flight of stairs to board the plane. This included slogging through slush where rock salt had thawed an overnight snowfall. I had packed my overcoat, expecting to be indoors until we landed. Talk about shock!

By the time we reached St. Louis, the temperature there had plummeted thirty degrees, accompanied by tornado warnings and a hailstorm vicious enough to break windshields. Welcome to the Midwest. But I have to admit that flying First Class in this instance was well worth the extra money, considering the strain that lay ahead.

The other trip, from New York to Barcelona, occurred six years ago. Daughter Aimee was getting married in Valros, France, and the family was gathering for the celebration. We were leaving on New Years Day, 2000, right in the middle of the Y2K computer scare. Would the plane fall from the sky?

Our reservations were strictly Coach, all the way. We hooked up with each other at JFK Airport for the overseas leg. When they called my name to come to the podium, I was puzzled. Had I lost something? No, they had chosen me at random for an upgrade.

How delightful! But there was only one seat, and this presented a dilemma. I was healthy. My ex-husband, who suffered a back injury in World War II, was already limping miserably. The trip would be excruciating for his large frame in a Coach seat. The swap was made, and he boarded first. I must admit to feeling pretty pious. That should cover all sins, past, present, and maybe a few in the future.

I squeezed into his old seat, which was, indeed, uncomfortable. A few minutes later a smiling flight attendant leaned over and whispered: "They reconfigured the First Class cabin. Would you like to come up and sit next to your ex-husband?" I was speechless. Fortunately we had exchanged Forgive and Forget letters a long time ago, or it might have taken several seconds to make up my mind.

Haleakaka Times, March 15, 2006

Rags To Riches

"Keep your head down. Keep your head down." The coach's mantra burned in his brain as he stepped to the ten yard line and loosened up with practice kicks. First game. First time in the lineup. New school. New sport. Could it get any more tense?

This whole football thing was new to him. It was his mom who convinced the coach to give him a tryout. "Maybe he can't throw. But watch him kick!"

The referee's whistle triggered an adrenaline rush. St. Anthony High School jayvees had just scored their first goal of the new season. It was up to him to put the extra point on the board. The teams squared off, cleats clawing into dry grass. The Trojans' quarterback grabbed the snap from center and slapped it onto the black tee.

This was it. Show-Me time. The boy in jersey Number Two took a deep breath, put his head down and belted one. Twenty yards, straight between the goal posts. He didn't need to look up. As the coach had said, the roar of the crowd told him. His first point in his first game for his new school.

Beaming, he trotted to the sidelines, where a teammate yanked open the helmet strap, something he couldn't do for himself. For this youngster had arrived in the world with birth defects, including limited use of his arms. Fifteen years ago, as a newborn, he had been rushed by air ambulance to Kapiolani Women's and Children's Hospital, in Honolulu, with life-threatening problems. There he had survived five surgeries, countless needles, and four and a half months of misery. At one point it took four nurses to hold him down while a feeding tube was inserted.

As he grew, the youngster learned to adjust. Fear was never a deciding factor. His middle name means "Forward!" With the encouragement of his parents, particularly his Mom, he learned to snow ski; he rode the Maui shore break on a skim board, wore out countless pairs of shoes skateboarding. Unable to extend his arms to break a fall, he endured repeated concussions. Soccer, hacky-sack, he played them all. Maybe he couldn't lace his boots, snap his helmet strap or throw a forward pass. But he could kick! And he practiced. And practiced. And practiced.

It all came together on that September day, when one fifteen-year-old showed the world that it's what you do, not what you can't do, that counts.

Was he afraid of getting hit on the football field? "No, Tutu. The only thing I was afraid of was missing the point after touchdown."

Tutu ? Oh, yes. That's Hawaiian for Grandma. And that's how come I know Zachariah Imua Platt. Only I call him Zach.

About the Author

Emily Ann O'Neil was born in New York City, N.Y., April 2, 1922. After a few years in Ridgefield Park, N.J., the family returned to her parents' home, St. Louis, MO. She grew up there, with two brothers and two sisters, and graduated from St. Louis University with a B.S. in English and an M.A. in American History. She was a staff writer for the Women's Page of the St. Louis Globe-Democrat for three years, and spent fifteen months as a novice with the Religious of the Sacred Heart.

She married Robert Alan Bott in 1951. They had seven children in ten years, and lived in Mt. Vernon and Northfield, IL., Birmingham, MI., Huntington, Long Island, N.Y., New Canaan, CT., and Grosse Pointe, MI. In 1970 Bob retired from young and Rubicam Advertising Agency, and the family moved to Maui that August. Divorce followed two years later.

She worked for the Sheraton (got fired), for KMVI Radio (got fired), as a substitute teacher at St. Anthony High School, as Polynesian Department head at Liberty House, and finally settled into a 25-year career as a Northwestern Mutual Life Insurance Co. agent. She took early retirement at age 77, and since then has done volunteer work: ushered at the Maui Arts and Cultural Center, been a wish granter for the Make-A-Wish organization, a Eucharistic minister at the hospital (got fired), and a 30-year, 5,000 hours volunteer in the Emergency Room at Maui Memorial Medical Center. There, her puppet Lambchop is better known than she is, and that's just fine with Lambchop.

*   *   *   *

This book is her 90th birthday presents to her kids, Brian, Eric, Kathy, Martha, Daniel, Aimee and Sarah. They are her crowning accomplishments. She rests on her laurels.

Made in the USA
Las Vegas, NV
12 September 2021

30153601R00056